jrock, ink. JOSEPHINE YUN

a concise report on 40 of the biggest rock acts in japan

Stone Bridge Press ▪ *Berkeley, California*

PUBLISHER   Stone Bridge Press
P.O. Box 8208, Berkeley, CA 94707
510-524-8732
sbp@stonebridge.com
www.stonebridge.com

ART DIRECTOR AND DESIGNER   Yelena Zhavoronkova
ILLUSTRATION ART DIRECTORS   Yelena Zhavoronkova, Artemy Lebedev
ILLUSTRATOR   Yana Moskaluk, © Art. Lebedev Studio

Printed in Singapore
10  9  8  7  6  5  4  3  2  1    2009  2008  2007  2006  2005

ISBN   1-880656-95-7

10 Introduction
20 Glossary
24 Nanase Aikawa
26 THE ALFEE
28 BOØWY
30 the brilliant green
32 BUCK-TICK
34 B'z
36 Cocco
38 Dir en grey
40 Duël le quartz
42 Duel Jewel
44 Gackt
46 GLAY
48 hide
50 Janne Da Arc
52 Judy And Mary
54 Kagrra,
56 Kuroyume
58 La'cryma Christi
60 L'Arc~en~Ciel
64 LOVE PSYCHEDELICO
68 LUNA SEA
72 Malice Mizer
76 Miyavi
78 Mr. Children
80 Penicillin
82 PIERROT
84 the pillows
86 Princess Princess
88 Psycho le Cému
90 Sheena Ringo
92 SADS
94 SEX MACHINEGUNS
96 SHAZNA
98 SHEENA & THE ROKKETS
100 Shonen Knife
102 Siam Shade
104 Takui
106 Thee Michelle Gun Elephant
108 Unicorn
110 X JAPAN
114 Discography

# Introduction

Q What is jrock?

A Jrock is short for Japanese rock. It's rock music produced in Japan.

On June 30, 1966, the Beatles played their first concert in Japan. It was held in Tokyo's Nippon Budokan, a martial arts hall built to honor Japan's war dead. Because of the hall's meaning and history—it had showcased martial arts exclusively—a mix of fans and protesters filled the streets, cheering or lamenting its deviation from the norm. The Beatles were sequestered in their hotel room, heavily guarded, and escorted wherever they went. But they sold out the Budokan (10,000 seats) for three consecutive days. That a group of shaggy-haired British hippies could sensationally succeed in a still-conservative country that had been an imperialist dictatorship just thirty years before showed how far Japan had come in absorbing Western culture. The protesters, on the other hand, showed how far it still had to go. Long a rigid, conformist society, the Japanese population's unquestioning submission to authority had permitted its involvement in World War II. With the post-war recovery came a renewal of popular interest in Western culture that had been sparked in the Meiji era. Every aspect of the Beatles—their 180-degree look, foreign loudness, and individualism, combined with an infectious musical style—alternately upset, ruffled, and fascinated the wholly polite Japanese. And it's not been the same since. The Beatles' Japanese contemporaries, a proliferation of image-friendly bands collectively labeled Group Sounds (GS), acclimated audiences further by covering songs by artists such as the Rolling Stones. The public was prepped, GS faded, and '70s rock traveled through a time warp before Japanese rock roots took hold. As it turned out, instead of merely experiencing a casual fad, some Japanese had been profoundly affected. The country had been swept by rock fever, but after the masses had gotten over it and moved on to the next big thing, an unshakable inspiration still raged in the hearts and fingers of a select few. For them, it proved to be more than love. These newly birthed rock groups made a go at an idol-packed, management-controlled industry in the 1970s. Though viewed as kitschy imitations by the public, folk rock groups like THE ALFEE (initially a cover band called Confidence) and punk rock hawkers such as SHEENA & THE ROKKETS (which also did covers) in fact laid the foundation for Japanese rock by emulating the

sound and look of their Western influences. Audiences weren't receptive at first, but persistence paid off. By 1981, SHEENA & THE ROKKETS had toured with Elvis Costello and the Ramones; by 1983, THE ALFEE had scored its first hit, "Marie Ann." The spirit of rock further spread in the early '80s underground with bands such as Shonen Knife (formed by bored office clerks), BOØWY (co-founded by an expelled high school student), and BUCK-TICK, whose members wore dramatic makeup and styled their hair sky-high. Unlike pop stars, these musicians made their own decisions; BOØWY was an early example of this and founded its own production company, Ø Connection, in 1984. Despite the absence of major label support, a fan base grew. By 1986, BOØWY's fifth album, *Beat Emotion*, sold its first million. In 1987, BUCK-TICK went major. And in 1988, BOØWY sold out two nights at the newly opened Tokyo Dome (95,000 tickets) in ten minutes. Though not entirely convinced, Japan was more rock-ready than before. So when a flamboyant, violent rock group called X (later known as X JAPAN) broke out of the indie scene on its own terms in 1989, there was a need to feed. X blistered past idols on the charts with consecutive No. 1 hits. It became the first modern rock group to be broadcast nationwide and the first Japanese band to fill Tokyo Dome for three consecutive days. Its members set up multiple record labels—Extasy, LEMONed, Platinum—to sign, foster, and promote new rock talent. Finally, though visually influenced by KISS and glam, X developed its own unique musical style and was fueled by a Japanese concept. Thus hooked, it was the definitive point at which the Japanese began looking to themselves for rock music, and Japan's first personal rock movement, visual kei, was born. A time lapse still existed between the United States and Japan in 1993. U.S. artists were into grunge, for example, making costuming seem outdated. In Japan, however, X JAPAN was still dressed to kill and topping the charts. X's appearance and its success broke off the first concrete, constant slab of wildly popular Japanese rock groups. Thee Michelle Gun Elephant carried all the traditions of raucous pub and punk rock. Dynamic duo B'z was the perfect partnership of ex-pop backup guitarist, to-be signature Gibson guitarist Tak Matsumoto and neurotic

math-tutor-cum-vocalist Koshi Inaba. As for visual kei, GLAY continued X JAPAN's elegantly tortured legacy, debuting with Extasy before going major, pulling in its own varied audience with its neither-pop-nor-rock music. By the late '90s, that self-reliance became even more evident with bands like L'Arc~en~Ciel, Judy And Mary, and Malice Mizer. After building their own fan base from scratch as indie bands, these groups gained widespread popularity by having their songs and likenesses featured in videogames, TV series, and animated series (anime). L'Arc~en~Ciel's first major hit, "Blurry Eyes," was used as an opening theme for the anime *DNA²*. Judy And Mary got its guns from "Sobakasu," a theme used for another series, *Rurouni Kenshin*. L'Arc set a record by taking up the No. 1 and No. 2 spots on the charts with two simultaneously released albums in 1999, *ark* and *ray*. Malice Mizer, a visual kei band that was gothic and classically European, influenced by Italian horror flicks, brought up the underground and went major after topping the indie charts in 1996. The group's elegant, effeminate second vocalist was a favorite base for videogame character designers at Squaresoft. Rock and Japanese mainstream media essentially tag-teamed each other, which led to the simultaneous containment and circulation of rock within Japan. As the new millennium approached, Japanese rock was operating on its own. The Fuji Rock Festival, founded in 1997, was in full swing, featuring a coveted array of international and domestic artists. International media began to take notice: Shonen Knife had already toured with Nirvana in 1993, but in 1998, the *New York Times* zoomed in on singer-songwriter Cocco at Austin's South by Southwest music festival; Thee Michelle Gun Elephant got rave reviews in the UK. In 2001, LOVE PSYCHEDELICO appeared at South by Southwest and even embarked on a U.S. mini-tour. A heightened interest in Asian culture that was being spread via animated movies, films, and the visual arts helped dispel a lingering prejudice against Japanese artists. But at twenty-five, Japanese rock had its own identity and was able to easily and convincingly absorb styles like grunge, as in the case of the trio the brilliant green. And in 2001, the brilliant green was listed in *Time* magazine alongside U2 and Radiohead as one of the top ten

bands on Earth. Meanwhile, anime was booming in the United States, and American mainstream music had dissolved into an amateur mess that was rehashed, whiny, and generic. Fans—not newspapers or magazines—clamored for anime, and subsequently, their soundtracks. Anime-centric conventions diversified, sporting panels and music video screenings of Japanese music, including rock. Along with voice actors, musical guests and composers of anime themes were invited to—and adored at—the conventions. A visual indie band called Duel Jewel appeared at Project A-Kon in Dallas in 2002, intriguing audiences even though it had never done anime work. In 2003, Sony Music Japan established an affiliate in southern California to promote and make accessible its Japanese artists in the United States. The following year, L'Arc~en~Ciel was welcomed in conjunction with the largest anime convention on the East Coast, Baltimore's Otakon, and made its North American debut, filling 12,000 seats. It rode not only the real-time success of its latest anime soundtrack hit "Ready Steady Go" from the series *Fullmetal Alchemist*, but on its work done for past series, which was discovered by international fans years later. Today, things are up to speed. Older Japanese rock is discovered through anime, videogames, and the Internet. Fans don't have to live in Japan to keep up with its rock scene, nor do Japanese need to wait to hear of goings-on in the West. But a smaller world doesn't translate into a loss of identity. Artists such as the multi-faceted Gackt, who has stressed the beauty and importance of Japanese lyrics, Kagrra,, whose music alludes to ancient Japan, and Sheena Ringo, avant-garde in integrating traditional Japanese elements, are examples of artists who make sure Japanese rock stays, well, Japanese. Rock has done an about face; it is coming home. Its acceptance and the acceptance of its messages still show how far societies have (or haven't) progressed. In Japan, the need to be different to succeed is great; for each innovative artist, throngs of imitators and emulators follow. Between walls of idols, a repressive social system, and greedy corporations, rock lives. SHEENA & THE ROKKETS are still around; B'z and LOVE PSYCHEDELICO are still influenced by the Beatles. VIVAROCK.

Chart rankings, record sales, sold-out performances at certain venues, and transitions from independent to major record labels are used to mark the milestones in artists' careers. Here, they may also be seen as marking the establishment and success of rock music in Japan. Rock runs directly counter to the stereotype of a passive, reserved, conformist Japan. With all the entertainment options available to the average consumer, it is surprising that rock gained any traction at all. The competition is largely domestic, consisting of the country's own pre-packaged pop acts and compilations of older acts. But Japanese rock is pitted against foreign artist releases as well. So, to blitz the record books in Japan is one thing; to do so as a Japanese rock act is something else completely. The visual kei band X JAPAN was based on the duality of human nature. Its concept was embodied by Yoshiki, the band's drummer and pianist, in the form of split-faced makeup, a half-spiked head of hair, and later, his makeup and dress as a woman. Beautiful men cross-dressing have long been a part of Japanese culture. For instance, after women were banned from Kabuki theater, men took over, playing the female as well as the male roles. Modern Japan thus has a historic familiarity with and basic acceptance of cross-dressing and male homosexuality whether implied or actual. While visual kei may have shocked due to its overdone look and loud, Western influence, its intent was wholly Japanese. You may find the orthography of band names, albums, and songs to be odd. Once English reaches Japan, it's as if all the rules are suspended. It, like rock, takes on new forms and meanings. Instead of following colons, for example, the subtitles of albums and songs are marked by tildes or hyphens. These have been left as is throughout the book. Many artists' names are initially written in katakana (the Japanese alphabet reserved for non-Japanese words) and are entirely capitalized when transitioning to English. In the case of Kagrra, (written with the comma), the comma denotes the band's status as a major label artist.

This book is organized alphabetically but reads from back to front in the Japanese style. Each artist or band occupies a two- or four-page spread. At the end of the book, you'll find a discography listing all the albums and mini-albums released by each artist (independent and major works are noted). This book strives to be current through Spring 2005. The forty artists selected for this book are, I believe, the best known across the diverse spectrum that is Japanese rock. They have played an essential role in the formation of the Japanese rock scene or a crucial part in its growth. They may have contributed to spreading the genre overseas and/or have continued to work despite the odds. My first exposure to jrock occurred when I was in high school, when an ad flashed on TV for THE ALFEE's Forest Hills, New York, concert. I was fascinated by the group's flair, and soon a color print from their *Nouvelle Vague* campaign was tacked to my bedroom wall. I didn't actually get my first aural taste of jrock until college, when a childhood friend introduced me to Japanese animation. One series I enjoyed was *Weiß Kreuz*, featuring voice actor Takehito Koyasu. An online profile of Koyasu listed his favorite band as L'Arc~en~Ciel. After attending Baltimore's Ota-kon and getting a huge kick out of the anime music videos, I found a Web site that hosted them for download. While scrolling through artists, I came across a video set to "Caress of Venus" by L'Arc~en~Ciel. I recognized the name, and opened it out of curiosity. The music was like nothing I had expected. An Internet search for more information on the band revealed how amazingly *beautiful* its members were. From there, I was introduced to Gackt. I listened to his "Saikai~Story~" and was stunned by the colors it evoked, and at how the guitars sounded like delicate fireworks. With the inspiration and help of such artists and their fans, I am pleased to present these notes on jrock. Through this book I hope to share my enthusiasm and admiration for the scene and its history.

SPECIAL THANKS  Gilles Poitras, Peter Goodman, Yelena Zhavoronkova, Yana Moskaluk, Ayako Willen,
Barry Harris

Bret McCabe, Lee Gardner, Andy O'Bannon, Marc Herman, Grace Liang,
Jessica Spinowitz, Gordon Wells, Gerald Tarrant, Elizabeth "Bunny" Switzer,
Kathy Chee, Justin Hart

Sawasdee Gackt dear.to/sawasdeegackt, Story: The Gackt Fan Website,
Shiroi Heya jrock.pitas.com, jrocknyc jrocknyc.blogspot.com,
The Senshi Gakuen www.senshigakuen.com

Ayano Kataoka and Family, Miyanaga-san, Takano-san,
Sachiko Uchida-Bennett, Samantha Landau, The Sato Family, The Panariello Family,
Julian Pellicano, James Stevenson, The Spinowitz Family, The Wunderbunnies,
Naoki Hirata, T.M. Revolution, Joanna Young, Jean Wilson, Jolie Lin, Kathryn Hayes,
Anthony Spano and Ana Rosner, Brian William Gish, Rain Noe, Vail Joy, Josh Kortbein,
Isaac Cates, Blake DePastino, Dale Keiger, Joanne Cavanaugh Simpson,
Greg Williamson, Carl Steadman, Tristan Davies, Chris Ford

Johns Hopkins University, Baltimore Symphony Orchestra, Baltimore *City Paper*,
Otakon, Anime Central, Stone Bridge Press, Art. Lebedev Studio,
Shogun Japanese Restaurant, Clayton & Co./Dark Sky Café

Centigrade-J www.centigrade-j.com, JRock Online www.jrockonline.com, Nihon-fr,
Project J www.projectj.net, The Pierrot HQ www.todokanai.net/ritz/pierrot

And many more fans, Web sites, friends, and family

ACKNOWLEDGMENTS

Tadashi Yokoshi (Columbia Music), Nobu Yamamoto (Pioneer), Sampei Yamaguchi (SMEJ), Naomi Yamada (SMEJ), Val, SWEET-HEART, Spike Sugiyama (Toshiba-EMI Ltd.), Atsushi Shibata (TOMATO HEAD), Michael Shelley (Confidential Recordings), Rie Sawaoka (SMEJ), Mr. Oishi (MAVERICK D.C., INC.), Yaz Noya (Tofu Records), Kazumi Noda (MAVERICK D.C., INC.), Mr. Nakazato (Columbia Music), Fumika Nagase (SMEJ), Koji Miyajima, Archie Meguro (SMEJ), Shojiro Matsuo (TOPLINE), Kaz Matsumoto (avex mode), Takeki Maeda (Nippon Crown), M-Farm, Harry Lo, Naomi Kurata (Universal Music), Yutaka Kubo (Nippon Crown), Maki Kawai (Victor), Yuji Kawaguchi (Victor), Tetsuya Iwasaki (Nippon Crown), Ken Isshiki (Toshiba-EMI Ltd.), Yuriko Inagaki (SMEJ), Kenichiro Ikeuchi, Ken-ichi Iida (MAVERICK D.C., INC.), Hiroto Hizume (Toshiba-EMI Ltd.), Yasuhiko Hasegawa (Universal Music), Hiroshi Hasegawa (Museum Museum), Sophie and Tim Collier, Yoshiko Asami (SMEJ), Heidi Anne-Noel (Girlie Action)

PHOTO CREDITS

Nanase Aikawa: avex mode
THE ALFEE: Toshiba-EMI Limited
Duel Jewel: M-Farm
Gackt: NIPPON CROWN & Museum Museum
Janne Da Arc: avex mode
Kuroyume: Toshiba-EMI Limited
Penicillin: avex mode
Psycho le Cému: NIPPON CROWN & SWEET-HEART
Sheena Ringo: Toshiba-EMI Limited
SEX MACHINEGUNS: Toshiba-EMI Limited
Shonen Knife: TOMATO HEAD

# Glossary

| | |
|---|---|
| GOLD DISK AWARDS | Prizes awarded based on the number of records an artist has sold. |
| KOTO | A traditional thirteen-stringed instrument resembling a zither with strings stretching the length of its sounding box. |
| LIVE | A live performance. Hence, clubs are also called "livehouses." |
| NAGOYA DIAMOND | Performance venue in Japan's third largest city. Capacity: 800. |
| NIHON RECORD TAISHO | Awarded since 1960; the Japanese equivalent of the Grammy. |
| NIHON YUUSEN TAISHO | Awarded since 1968; the Japanese equivalent of a Listener's Choice Award. |
| NIPPON BUDOKAN | A martial arts hall used as a performance venue. Capacity: 10,000–14,000. Also where the Beatles first performed in Japan. |
| ORICON CHARTS | Abbreviation of Original Confidence; the Japanese equivalent of the Billboard Music Charts. Divided into indie single, indie album, major single, and major album categories. |
| RED AND WHITE MUSIC FESTIVAL | Also known as the Red and White Singing Contest, "Kouhaku Uta Gassen" in Japanese, this end-of-year music event has been televised nationally since 1950 on NHK, Japan's government-run television channel. Performers are divided into two teams, Red and White, hence the name. |
| TOKYO DOME | The largest performance venue in Japan. Capacity: 55,000–56,000. |
| VISUAL KEI | Literally "visual style." A movement influenced by glam rock and traditional Japanese culture such as Kabuki theater, popularized in Japan by the rock band X (later known as X JAPAN) in the mid-1980s. Often based on a concept addressing or representing human nature, duality, or the shortcomings of society and fueled by conflict or pathos. Marked by heavy makeup, cross-dressing, and elaborate presentation. Musical elements vary; the look is more prominent, hence the name "visual style." |
| YOKOHAMA ARENA | Performance venue in Japan's largest seaport city. Capacity: 17,000. |

# Nanase Aikawa

vocals

SUPPORTING MEMBERS various
DATES 1994–

Gas station attendant. Gang member. Transfer student. High school dropout. Singer Nanase Aikawa's childhood metamorphoses were anything but idyllic (her name means "seven seas"). When she was fifteen, she entered a singing contest and lost. But she caught the attention of scout/producer Tetsuro Oda. As the story goes, he flew to Osaka specifically to sign Aikawa; she refused, but kept his card. Later, she changed her mind, contacted Oda, and moved to Tokyo at the age of nineteen. At twenty, Aikawa burst onto the scene with her first single, "Yume Miru Shoujo Ja Irarenai" (Don't Want To Be a Dreaming Girl) in 1995. The following year, her debut album, *Red*, sold 2 million copies in its first month. Her follow-up, 1997's *Paradox*, won best rock album of the year at the Eleventh Gold Disk Awards. Since then, Aikawa has released two albums, a mini-album, and two compilations and sold over 12 million copies. Her first best-of compilation album, *ID*, released in 1999, and 2000's *Foxtrot* both grabbed the No. 1 spot on the Japanese charts; *ID* also took home an award for Best Rock Album of the Year. Aikawa's singing is rough around the edges—a gutsy alto that's more cutting than cute—and her musical style tends to sound pop-rock. Sampling and tough techno abound around a standard rock setup that grooves, and low-key numbers like "Crying" and "Sakurasaku" (Blooming Sakura) balance amplified ballads like "China Rose." "midnight blue" jumps and pumps with nonstop energy, laced with wicked guitar; "SEVEN SEAS" opens grandly before turning into a rollicking, winsome number with spates of churning guitar. And Aikawa's look has changed from black to blonde to red and back again. Her pretty face, combined with her husky, roguish voice, has fans calling her everything from "Queen of Rock" to a "rock goddess."

Aikawa has a bit of rock royalty from Japan and abroad in her court. In 2000, she switched producers to Tomoyasu Hotei, former guitarist of BOØWY. Ex-Megadeth guitarist Marty Friedman joined her band; so did bassist Natchin (formerly Natin of Siam Shade). Keyboard whiz I.N.A co-produced the 2003 single "Shock of Love." And Aikawa still receives rave reviews at Friedman's Web site on a regular basis. Whatever the prerequisites to becoming a rock star are, Nanase Aikawa fulfilled them long ago. In addition to her musical career, Aikawa—who is a mother—balances out her badassedness by writing children's books, releasing *Boku wa Kujira* (I Am a Whale) and *Kujira Santa* (Whale Santa) in 2002. She is also known affectionately as Nana-chan.

# THE ALFEE

MEMBERS   Kohnosuke Sakazaki (guitar, vocals, percussion),
Toshihiko Takamizawa (guitar, vocals), Masaru Sakurai (bass, vocals)
DATES   1974–

It's always hard to break into the music business. But try doing it when the music you play hasn't really been done before, when it's without precedent or an established audience. THE ALFEE—singer/percussionist Kohnosuke Sakazaki, guitarist Toshihiko Takamizawa, and bassist Masaru Sakarai—initially got together in high school as a cover band called Confidence. They would need plenty of guts and faith to do what they wished. THE ALFEE appeared quietly on the scene in 1974. It took nine years of uncertainty, including two hit single attempts, two different record labels, and freelance work (which got them on the Red and White Music Festival as a backing band for a pop singer) before a single, "Marie Ann," scored in 1983. Its members' next goal was to play Nippon Budokan, which they achieved that August. (With just one hit, it was a deal.) At the end of the year, Sakurai, Sakazaki, and Takamizawa returned to play in the Music Festival—by themselves. Visually, THE ALFEE is a terrific trio. With sky-high cheekbones and super-flair hair, princely Takamizawa is coolly flamboyant à la Jonny Greenwood of Radiohead. Sakurai, always in a suit and shades, resembles a bass-playing gangster. Sakazaki used to sport a prominent Afro, but the times they are a-changin'. All members have retained their look, aging well. Catchy, fun, big, they know how to put on a show, and that showmanship is reflected in their songs. Musically, THE ALFEE arrived at a compromise: Sakurai loved folk music, a fan of Simon and Garfunkel and Crosby, Stills, Nash & Young (this is especially evident in THE ALFEE's earlier work). Takamizawa wanted to slide electric. The result is music that's simultaneously melodious and plugged in. Their music has graduated from mellow folk tunes to synthed-up, elaborate, over-the-top affairs: think power choruses and charged-up singalong numbers, zany and complicated. Frilled with acoustic guitar and piano, it's all held together by the members' perfectly harmonized vocals. In 1991, THE ALFEE appeared on the American Music Awards. It performed at Forest Hills Stadium, New York, in 1998 as part of its *Nouvelle Vague* tour; the concert was also a benefit for victims of that year's Kobe earthquake. In 2001, the single "Juliet" entered the Oricon at No. 5. And 2004 marked the thirtieth anniversary of its first major label release. Hardly victims of late-career bloat and sloppiness in any department, THE ALFEE's members are still in business, slick and steady. With over forty albums under their belts, they've proven themselves victors over the odds in the long haul. And in a business that destroys so many artists before they even begin, they have earned much respect for their perseverance—for having started and stayed.

# BOØWY

| | |
|---|---|
| MEMBERS | Kyosuke Himuro (vocals), Tomoyasu Hotei (guitar), Matsui Tsunematsu (bass), Makoto Takahashi (drums) |
| EX-MEMBERS | Kazuaki Fukasawa (saxophone), Atsushi Moroboshi (guitar), Mamoru Kimura (drums) |
| DATES | 1981–1988 |

When someone has a mind of his own, it usually gets him into trouble. BOØWY (pronounced "boy," meaing "tyrant" in Japanese) was all about trouble. After Tomoyasu Hotei was expelled from high school (he allegedly talked back to a teacher) and moved to Tokyo, he was contacted by rival band member Kyosuke Himuro. In 1981, BOØWY was formed when four other members—saxophonist Kazuaki Fukasawa, guitarist Atsushi Moroboshi, bassist Tsunematsu Matsui, and drummer Makoto Takahashi—were picked up through auditions. Hotei played lead guitar; Himuro sang. Fukasawa and Moroboshi left after debut album *Moral*—a punky, snarky, attitudinized piece of work à la the Clash with clean, clever music that's tight and quirky like Talking Heads—but the foursome BOØWY continued operating and set up its own production company, Ø Connection. *Just A Hero* sports souped-up, energetic synth work and quavering, wavy guitar. *Instant Love* is peppered with quick metallic waves of both, Himuro's hushed vocals echoing seductively like

David Bowie's crooning in *Labyrinth*. And BOØWY gave rock a cool face in Japan. Towering, slim Hotei looked (and still looks) like a lean, mean anime villain; pretty boy Himuro would posture and pout, sunken-cheeked and saturnine. BOØWY became one of Japan's first widely popular rock bands, and its reach didn't end there. It played London's historic Marquee Club (where the Rolling Stones played their first ever gig) in 1985. In 1986, *Beat Emotion* reflected the growing receptiveness of rock music in Japan, becoming BOØWY's first million seller. In 1987, *Psychopath* took off at 800,000 copies. And for its two-night farewell concert in 1988, BOØWY went out by selling out 95,000 seats in ten minutes to a just-opened Tokyo Dome; scalpers wanted ¥500,000 (about US$4,000 at the time) per ticket. Even after BOØWY disbanded, its members have enjoyed sustained successes as solo artists. In 1996, Hotei appeared at Nippon Budokan as a guest of David Bowie and performed at the closing ceremonies of the Atlanta Olympic Games with composer Michael Kamen. He's also showed up in a UNESCO concert lineup alongside Bon Jovi, INXS, and Bob Dylan. He's written and performed music to several movie soundtracks, including *Fear and Loathing in Las Vegas* (1998), *Samurai Fiction* (1998), and *Kill Bill Vol. 1* (2003), and covered songs by artists ranging from Led Zeppelin to hide with Spread Beaver. Himuro's persuasive voice, meanwhile has earned him a place as one of Japan's best-selling solo artists; all of his albums and singles have landed no lower than the Oricon's top five spots. Not bad for a pair of punks.

# the brilliant green

MEMBERS Tomoko Kawase (vocals), Ryo Matsui (guitar), Shunsaku Okuda (bass)
SUPPORTING MEMBERS various
DATES 1995–

Yellow and blue make green. Mix together Shunsaku Okuda, Tomoko Kawase, and Ryo Matsui, though (favorite colors: blue, red, and gray, respectively), and you get the brilliant green. Formed in Kyoto when high school classmates Okuda and Matsui scouted would-be model/MTV veejay "Tommy" (as Tomoko is known) from a local club, "BuriGuri" (as it's nicknamed in Japan) first turned out a few good demo tapes that garnered the attention of major record labels. Its subsequent and self-produced debut, 1997's all-English single "Bye Bye Mr. Mug," made a local splash. A second single, "goodbye and good luck," was also warmly received. But it was BuriGuri's third single—"There will be love there~ai no aru basho~" (There will be love there~the place where love is~)—that dazzled. After entering the Oricon singles chart at No. 14, "There will be love there" climbed to No. 1 in seven weeks, became the theme song to a TV series, and went double platinum. In 1998, the trio's self-titled, full-length debut *the brilliant green* shot to No. 2 on the charts and went platinum in two *days*. The group continued its No. 1 singles streak with "Sono Speed de" (With This Speed), which became the theme for another TV series. And in 1999, sophomore album *TERRA2001* matched *tbg*, clocking in at No. 2 on the albums chart. BuriGuri's music is versatile: easy listening for either a summer drive or a tear-jerky rainy day. With a touch of the Beach Boys and faint hints of the Goo Goo Dolls, it grooves securely, rumbly rough but softened oft by the timbre of Tommy's vocals. And Tommy's voice is like the wispy, smoke-tendriled aftermath of a time bomb. Candy-dusted, sprightly or somber, even indignant at times, her airy cooing is reminiscent of Leigh Nash or breathy Donna Lewis. Together, the trio is like the Cardigans crushed with Veruca Salt. *TERRA2001*'s follow-up, *Los Angeles*, is pure, straight-up grunge with gunning, blistering guitars, Tommy's vocals metallic—and in 2001, it landed the trio a spot in *Time* magazine among U2, Radiohead, and Portishead as one of the top ten bands on the planet. BuriGuri then went on hiatus until 2002, as Tommy pursued multiple solo projects. Its comeback, *THE WINTER ALBUM*, was released in December 2002. Now at a decade together, the brilliant green is experienced, and its music, like its name, has proven to be anything but dully monochromatic.

# BUCK-TICK

MEMBERS  Atsushi Sakurai (vocals), Hisashi Imai (guitar), Hidehiko "Hide" Hoshino (guitar, keyboard), Yutaka "U-ta" Higuchi (bass), Toll Yagami (drums)

EX-MEMBER  Araki (vocals)

DATES  1983–

Once upon a time, around a school kid hangout far, far away, a rock band was born. The hangout was a convenience store run by the family of guitarist Hisashi Imai, the band, BUCK-TICK, whose beginnings included Araki on vocals, Atsushi on drums, Hisashi on guitar, guitarist and keyboardist Hide (short for Hidehiko), and bassist U-ta. Initially dubbed Hinan Go-Go (Criticism Go-Go), they first began playing at festivals as a cover band, dressed entirely in suits. In 1984, Hisashi renamed the band "baku chiku" (firecracker) with the English spelling BUCK-TICK. It played at a Yamaha-sponsored contest, still in suits but this time with all original work. The following year, it debuted live at Tokyo hotspot Shinjuku Jam. Araki left, Atsu-shi became vocalist, and Toll Yagami, U-ta's jaded older brother, filled in on drums, albeit skeptically. The new BUCK-TICK played in December 1985, again at Shinjuku Jam, and then was scouted by and signed to an indie label. A fan-club newsletter was in print by that November. After the release of indie debut *HURRY UP MODE*—the first indie album on CD in Japan—and a tour, it went major with a celebratory gig in June 1987. BUCK-TICK became known for, well, looking weird and acting crazy. Its visual trademark was its members' gravity-defying hair. It played a secret live event in January 1988 under the name BLUCK-TLICK; a comic book, *Hearts*, came out that July. (The storyline centered on a struggling rock band modeled after BUCK-TICK called BLUCK-TLICK and its members all had the same first names as BUCK-TICK members.) In August, BUCK-TICK announced that from then on, its members would wear its hair up only when it wanted to—despite management's protests. An autumn sojourn/recording session in the UK began the band's love affair with London, and the foreign influence continued even as BUCK-TICK seemed to examine its roots. *Aku no Hana* (Evil Flowers), released in 1990, contained more Japanese lyrics and was BUCK-TICK's first Japanese-titled album, but it was inspired by Baudelaire's *Les Fleurs du Mal*. A remix album, *Shapeless*, featured photos from the band's trip to Istanbul. With *Darker Than Darkness*, BUCK-TICK became one of the first bands to use a bonus track feature; confused consumers returned album copies to stores, thinking them defective. BUCK-TICK's music is smashed-together nuances of everything from Depeche Mode and New Order to U2 and the Knack. While wry, it can float and be nebulously melodic. *Mona Lisa Overdrive* is stimulating in an electronically layered, busy way; overall, its repertoire is volatile, industrial synth rock, crushing and noisy, alarmingly obtrusive and dark. Masked in eye makeup, Atsushi looks and sounds possessed. BUCK-TICK was (and continues to be) an anomaly in the Japanese music scene, a tangle of goth rock diluted with synth and electronica. It's unhappy, dirty music, the musical equivalent of exploded soot and smoke.

# B'z

| | |
|---|---|
| MEMBERS | Koshi Inaba (vocals), Takahiro "Tak" Matsumoto (guitar) |
| SUPPORTING MEMBERS | various |
| DATES | 1988– |

B'z is big. The bestselling, bona fide jrock powerhouse (pronounced "beez") got its name from its two favorite artists, the Beatles and Led Zeppelin, and in Japan has enjoyed about as much (possibly more) success. But you wouldn't know it by the low profile the duo, vocalist Koshi Inaba and guitarist Tak Matsumoto, keeps offstage. As a general rule, unlike many other contemporary music acts, B'z doesn't do commercials or dramas. B'z was created when Matsumoto, who was already in the industry but wanted his own band, took a chance on then–sandwich maker/math tutor Inaba. After a fast-food job and a stint as a backing guitarist for the pop band TM Network, he got to hear Inaba's singing and arranged to meet him. With a few Beatles duets, Matsumoto and Inaba clicked; in September 1988 B'z was born. Two years later, the single "Taiyou no Komachi Angel" (Angelic Beauty from the Sun) became its first No. 1 hit on the Japanese charts. It wouldn't be the group's last. Every single released since then—thirty-something singles over fourteen years—has plowed through to No. 1 without fail, and so have all ten of its following albums. In 1998, compilations *Pleasure* and *Treasure*, released four months apart, easily sold 5 million copies each. And in 2003, the re-release of those same singles, paired with the release of a new one ("IT'S SHOWTIME!!"), packed spots Nos. 1–11 on the singles chart, an unprecedented feat. When not rewriting record books, B'z is booked—for superman tours spanning forty, fifty, even seventy concerts. With those kinds of schedules, it's hard to believe Inaba and Matsumoto would have time to play overseas, but they have recently begun to do just that as their popularity continues to spread. In 2001 the two went to Taiwan and Hong Kong, and in 2002 they played Los Angeles and San Diego, California. B'z then went on a six-stop North American tour in the fall of 2003, playing Las Vegas, San Francisco, Seattle, and Vancouver. Whether demure or dynamic, B'z is transfixing. It smacks a bit of Aerosmith, backed by synthesizer and sliced-up sampling. Inaba even sounds like Steven Tyler at times (especially when his vocals are harmonized), Freddie Mercury at others, changing from mellow and velvety to nasal and naughty. Tall and willowy, he transforms into a convulsing frontman onstage, a slack-kneed, quiver-quavering magnet. Mullet-sprouting Matsumoto, built like a tank, adds to the intensity with beefy guitar, feeding songs that are not only singable, but stompworthy and full of energy. Remarkably, for being awash in fame and fans, B'z remains cool, levelheaded, and polite, shrugging modestly. But with over 86 million records sold, a fanclub enrollment over half a million strong (possibly the largest in Japan), and a still-vibrant career, the buzz surrounding and produced by B'z will likely reverberate for a long while.

# Cocco

vocals

SUPPORTING MEMBERS various

DATES 1996–2001

Emphatic, enigmatic, paradoxical singer-songwriter Cocco, the camera-shy nature lover from Okinawa, disliked the music business. Yet, she did so much. She produced the artwork for her own CD covers and had English translations printed alongside Japanese lyrics (or vice versa). Cocco's debut was a self-titled, three-song indie EP in 1996, which included the single "Sing a Song~No Music, No Life~"—a cheery, "Hand In My Pocket"–like number. "Sing a Song" was plucked by Tower Records Japan as a theme to its commercials (in which Cocco also appeared) and was also redistributed in the United States. In 1997, Cocco performed at Austin's South by Southwest music festival and signed to a major label shortly thereafter. Her first major release, "Countdown," flipped the hourglass of her musical career that spring. Her first album, *Bouganvillea*, arrived in May 1997. Her second single, "Tsuyoku Hakanai Monotachi" (The Strong and Ephemeral), sold 200,000 copies on its November release. Sophomore album *Kumuiuta* followed in 1998, and it was during touring for *Kumuiuta* that Cocco began to tire of exposure. Already, her music had been made to complement her hard-hitting, inward lyrics. In a 2000 interview, she compared music-making to "shitting" and her albums to "shit"—not due to their quality, but because the process expelled the pent-up negativity and waste within her. Further, she dreaded appearing on TV, being misinterpreted, and feeling responsible for obsessive fans. Compared both to Fiona Apple (by the *New York Times*) and Alanis Morrisette (elsewhere), Cocco's widely varied style, in fact, is all her own. Her singing ranges from innocent piping to open-throated serenading; on *Bouganvillea*, she is a young siren, sprightly but deep. Her music runs from Bon Jovi–ish pop-rock to Nine Inch Nails–esque machinations with Tori Amos vocals. Strings, piano, bombastic drums and messes of guitar, marimba, tambourine, and a recorder all appear in her songs. In 2000, Cocco's third album, *Rapunzel*, climbed to No. 1 on the Oricon. A fourth album, *Sangrose*, was released in 2001. But after *Sangrose*, the clock ran out. Cocco announced her retirement and went home. Since then, she has continued to conduct business on her own terms, creating and making appearances that she feels comfortable with, and harnessing her fame to aid the cleaning of Okinawa's beaches. Between two art books, a documentary of her personal cleanup effort, *Heaven's Hell*, was released in 2003. In 2004, she re-recorded "Sing a Song~ No Music, No Life~" for Tower Records' twenty-fifth anniversary, tweaking the subtitle to "No Music, No Love Life."

# Dir en grey

MEMBERS   Kyo (vocals), Die (guitar), Kaoru (guitar), Toshiya (bass), Shinya (drums)
DATES     1997–

Dir en grey isn't Marilyn Manson, nor is it Tool, despite often being lumped with the looks of one and grouped with the intent of the other. And if you've ever tried to label Dir en grey accordingly, there's a good chance that it's screaming about you—or someone just like you. After bassist Kisaki left indie band La:Sadies in 1997, the remaining members picked up new bassist Toshiya, forming Dir en grey (Deg for short). Its name means "two sides of a coin" (in a combination of German, French, and English) and refers to two-faced human nature. After an auspicious start—its first single, "I'll," broke the sales record for indie singles in 1998—Deg was scouted by former X JAPAN member/producer Yoshiki at a Tokyo club. Yoshiki went on to produce three singles that, released simultaneously, became the band's major debut. All of the songs broke into the Oricon's top ten spots and were featured on Deg's first full-length album, 1999's *GAUZE*. Four albums and a mini-album later, Deg's writhing music is like its name: disturbingly melodic, grotesquely adept. Threaded with wrecking guitar, it is melodically dissonant—sometimes twisted around a Brahms dance, Gregorian chant, or clips of dialogue, political speeches, and domestic abuse—off-kilter with odd, halting rhythms blossoming inexplicably into melancholic, bittersweet choruses. Kyo's voice is throaty, hollow, and sullen; alternately, he unleashes staccato, ear-tearing screeches like a demonic banshee. Deeply entrenched, Deg's work engulfs a wide range of mostly dark emotions one can get lost in, swallowing listeners in a black avalanche of haunting music both restless and relentless. Like its music, Deg's look has tossed and turned in the years following its debut. Initially, it continued in the tradition of visual kei with extravagant makeup, violet-blue hair, and Shinya as its auburn-tressed, red-mouthed cross-dresser. That image has since changed from flamboyant and colorful to menacing, smoldering, and dark. Ultimately, however, it is Deg's concept that hooks fans. Deg studies society closely, and its music is a response to, a reflection of, and a protest against the hatred that society generates. (As a result, Kyo's lyrics never end happily.) It is also one of few jrock bands to respond to a growing demand worldwide. Legions of fans from all over the globe flock to Japan to support Dir en grey—and in 2004, the band's management responded in kind, coordinating travel packages for overseas fans that allowed them to easily reserve tickets for and fly to Deg concerts. Also in 2004, it opened an English section at its official Web site. But Deg has far to go. Says a missive on the band's Web site: "Until the day comes where there is no more hurt in this world, [the members of] Dir en grey will carry the emotions of hurt and sorrow in their music, and they will continue to scream."

# Dué le quartz

MEMBERS   Sakito (vocals), Miyabi (guitar), Kikasa (bass), Kazuki (drums)
EX-MEMBER   Ken (guitar)
DATES   1998-2002

Spikes. Vinyl. Indigo hair. Leather. Lace. Japanese indie band Dué le quartz (translation: two-sided crystal) knew how to dress, and its music wasn't too bad, either. In the dogfight of an indie scene, its young and energetic members scooped up fandom not only in their conceptual emulation of X JAPAN (the crystal represents human nature), but with their own engaging personalities and fantastic, immaculately elaborate image. Dué was formed in December 1998 by Sakito and Ken, and in February 1999 began gigging around Tokyo. That April, it appeared on the popular TV show Pa Pa Pa Pa Puffy! hosted by jpop duo Puffy AmiYumi. New guitarist Miyabi joined the line-up in June after Ken left in May. It was a good addition. On 2000's *Jisatsu Ganbou* (Suicidal Wish), a music box welcomes listeners before becoming distorted and vinegary, expertly escorting them to tight, thrashing drums and a shrill, poisonous energy. Ghoulish wailing and catchy, tragic melodies are darkly memorable, with plenty of dissonance and twisted distortion. Sakito's sometimes flat, sometimes out-there vocals aren't stellar but suit the music well, adding to the pathos. There's fairy barking, and an aural walk through chilly, hollow environs ending in a violent crunch of fruit—you'll never look at apples the same way again. Bursts of backup screeching imply that Miyabi's teeth are far sharper than should be legal; rhythmic interludes are headbangable, yet singably melodic. And then there was its dress. Dué le quartz's members were elegantly garbed in everything from straps, collars, and studded belts and bodices to suits, silver fur-trimmed hats, and pieces of heavily embroidered fabric, feathers and flowers wound into their colored hair. Slim, styled, and made-up, nearly all the members were genderless. In 2002, Kikasa left Dué le quartz, and the band broke up that September. Kikasa stinted with Shelly Trip Realize before forming a new band with Sakito, FIGURE, with Kazuki on support drums; Miyabi went solo, changing his name to Miyavi. Despite this, Dué le quartz and its caustic, shredding-yet-beautiful music still glitters as a classic example of second-generation visual kei in the Japanese indie firmament.

# Duel Jewel

MEMBERS    Hayato (vocals), Shun (guitar), Yuya (guitar), Natsuki (bass), Val (drums)
EX-MEMBERS    Psy (guitar), Takashi (guitar), Ka-non (bass)
DATES    1997–

Indie band Duel Jewel is young, but it's already accomplished something other groups only dream of: performing in the United States. Singer Hayato, guitarist Shun, and drummer Val—who have been together since high school—floated through a fragmented history full of starts and stops, fleeting (or missing) members, and other hindrances, until, in 2001, a post in English on the band's Web site set up its first American live. In 2002, bassist Natsuki joined the band just before it followed through, debuting at the Project A-Kon convention in Dallas, Texas. There, it brought a jaggedly talented mix of melodiousness, intense, complex drumming, and rad guitar. Sweet, swooning ballads like "Tsuki to tawamure" (Flirting with the moon) have Hayato's trembling voice sounding like Elvis. "Etsu" (Rapture) begins with Shun's searing guitar before melding into furious drumming and revolving bass. And "Paranoid Trash" throws you headfirst into a super-tight, high-speed headbanging spell. Duel Jewel became the first visual kei band to perform in the United States in conjunction with the rising popularity of anime, and the attendant scene at conventions dedicated to anime. It returned to play a con circuit, performing at similar festivals in Virginia, Chicago, and Los Angeles. Unlike the many ventures of other underground jrock bands into the United States, an all-ages audience experienced Duel Jewel as part of these events—as another aspect of Japanese culture—making the multi-faceted spectacle more accessible. The band opened the eyes, if not the ears, of a new audience with its spiked hair, vivid presentation, and Hayato's dazzling charm. But an overseas debut will only get you so far. After each stint (a recent one being Houston's Onicon in 2004), Duel Jewel returns to the same scene in Japan that it left—an overcrowded, competitive indie beat. Stateside, it had the stage to itself, whereas in Japan, as many as five or six bands will play the same club in one evening, their slots limited to roughly twenty minutes each. And should Duel Jewel attain its ultimate goal of becoming pro, the camaraderie and flexibility it enjoys as an indie band may dim. Still, its members will do their best. In the vast sea of Japanese rock, Duel Jewel is a glimmer, with time to shine.

# Gackt

vocals, guitar, piano

SUPPORTING MEMBERS You (guitar, violin), Yukihiro "Chachamaru" Fujimura (guitar), Ryu (drums)
EX-SUPPORT MEMBERS Masa (guitar), Ren (bass, cello), Toshi (drums)
DATES 1999–

Gackt is everywhere. Model, actor, author, love doctor, quirky comic—but above all, he is a consummate musician, and even in that field, his abilities are multifold. Gackt began his career playing guitar, piano, drums, and an array of brass instruments in addition to being blessed with a velvet voice. After a job working in a casino and a stint as drummer/vocalist of a small-time indie band, Gackt was the princely frontman of visual group Malice Mizer from 1995 to 1998. It was during his reign as vocalist that MM released its second album *Voyage* and its major debut, *merveilles*. In 1999, he went solo, assembled a backup band, and flew to the United States to record. His mini-album *Mizerable* placed at No. 2 on the Oricon that May. *MARS* (2000) and *Rebirth* (2001), both full-length works, each climbed to No.3. Gackt has a talent for orchestration and for blending classical elements into the rock genre. Castanets, chimes, harpsichord, timpani, oboe, and marimba are sprinkled across his albums, and his style ranges from romantically classical to experimental and unfolding progressive rock. *Rebirth*'s "4th" is hair-blowingly operatic, with Gackt singing in a stunning falsetto. *MOON's* somber, violet-colored "Fragrance" sports a sitar; "memories," also on *MOON*, closes with an all-out orchestral score, the highlight of which is a pristine piano solo radiating the infinite warmth of a Chopin concerto. Samples upon electronic samples are another Gackt trademark: another *Rebirth* track, "uncontrol," is a pulsing, throttling, nuts-and-bolts piece that morphs into a static-peppered, high-energy chorus. And there are few limits to his experimentation. Gackt completely rewrote and rerecorded his most popular singles for compilation albums *The Sixth Day* and *The Seventh Night*, making them more than just remastered releases. A self-proclaimed perfectionist, he writes all of his music and lyrics to quality, not quantity—a trait that always has his fans clamoring for the next work. Gackt's presence and popularity continues to spread, inspire, and charm. In 2003, he starred in the movie *Moon Child* (which he co-wrote) with L'Arc~en~Ciel vocalist hyde; the movie was shown at the Philadelphia Film Festival in 2004 and was scooped up for a U.S. release. He was mentioned on National Public Radio's *All Things Considered* in April 2004, and after years of debate over whether or not Final Fantasy characters were based on him (or vice versa), a videogame, Bujingai—whose main character was designed after him—was released that July. All of this may have propelled him to near-idol status. But Gackt is a musician—and a rather sensitive one—at heart.

# GLAY

MEMBERS Teru (vocals), Hisashi (guitar), Takuro (guitar, keyboard/piano), Jiro (bass)
SUPPORTING MEMBERS D.I.E. (keyboard), Toshimitsu "Toshi" Nagai (drums)
EX-MEMBERS Akira (drums), Nobumasa (drums)
DATES 1988–

GLAY—the band that's not black or white, hard or soft, rock or pop—was formed in 1988 by vocalist Teru and guitarists Takuro and Hisashi. It began to seriously consider a career in music after it performed at Teru's sister's wedding in February 1990. The tears elicited at that event thanks to its song "Zutto Futari de" (Always together) became GLAY's motivation to wholeheartedly pursue music; it wanted to have that effect on more people. GLAY's members moved to Tokyo, but there was one problem: In a black-and-white scene, GLAY (the Japanese pronunciation of "gray") couldn't be categorized. Rowdy houses rejected it because its image wasn't hardcore enough; clubs carrying pop music turned them away, saying GLAY's music was too rough or hard. Finally, when bassist Jiro joined in 1992 ("I want to do something like Guns n' Roses," he said), GLAY changed its look with makeup and dramatic clothing—that sort of thing was acceptable by then—and the visual rock element gelled. A year later, it caught the attention of Yoshiki, founder of X JAPAN and indie label Extasy Records. Following its first album with Extasy, *Hai to Daiyamondo* (Ash and Diamond), GLAY went major in 1995 and released *SPEED POP*, which reached No. 8 on the Oricon. "Zutto Futari de," which had decided the band's path years before, became the theme for two TV programs. Then, in 1996, *BEAT out!* sprinted to No. 1, and *BELOVED*, released later that year, followed suit, going platinum. GLAY went on to become one of Japan's hugest rock bands thanks to its vast range of sound, image, and style. And its following has yet to wane; after five more albums, 2004's *THE FRUSTRATED* entered the charts at No. 2. GLAY's musical style is a fluid compromise between pop and punk rock. Between Sex Pistols–influenced Hisashi and ballad fan Takuro, who writes most of the group's music, GLAY is both gutsy and lyrical. Teru doesn't whine or scream; he carries a tune plainly, with strong, manly vocals. His low, slightly husky tenor has an easy, mellow, feel-good dimension, backed by whip-smart, clever music that is like rain. "However" is a partly sunny ballad, warmed by piano and strings. But "Sen no Knife ga Mune wo Sasu" (A Thousand Knives Pierce My Heart) stings, freezing with waspish guitar and drum set before easing to a light, blurry drizzle. So float, groove, and coast. Full of spiffy guitar riffs yet tender, it's motley, well-molded pop rock that keeps its fans—as the maxim goes—glad to be GLAY.

# hide

vocals, guitar, bass

SUPPORTING MEMBER  I.N.A (synth, programming)

DATES  1993–1998

Guitarist, solo artist, label founder, and collaborator hide (pronounced hee-day, spelled in lowercase) is one of the most tragic figures—and continues to be one of the most influential—in Japanese music. Born Hideto Matsumoto, he was moved by KISS, and in high school formed his first band, Saver Tiger. It was banned from the school, so it went to Tokyo to practice, playing small venues there. After Saver Tiger broke up, he subsequently received a phone call from Yoshiki, leader of X (later known as X JAPAN). In 1987, he became one of X's two guitarists. Fluorescent-haired and gaudily garbed, hide's stage persona was insolent, in your face, taunting, and belligerent, and it thrilled Japanese youth while horrifying older generations. Many Japanese felt stifled by convention and identified with his naughty rebelliousness; he became a cult figure. All the members of X JAPAN were unique, but hide continued to act out and dress up, standing apart visually after the other members had let their hair down. Still, hide's generous nature belied his outrageous look. While in X JAPAN, he scouted next-generation rock group LUNA SEA for Extasy. In 1994, he released *Hide Your Face*, followed by 1996's *Psyence*. Also in 1996, he founded his own production company, LEMONed, to jumpstart indie bands, believing the systematic, ultra-competitive road to the major leagues to be unfairly steep. He also became known for his donations to and special treatment of leukemia patients. After X JAPAN's breakup, hide went on to collaborate with various artists. In January 1998, he formed Tokyo-based Spread Beaver with a clutch of industry pillars including former X JAPAN bandmate Pata and Kiyoshi of Media Youth; his Stateside, industrial-metal project, Zilch, attracted guitarist Ray McVeigh (ex-Professionals), bassist Paul Raven (ex-Killing Joke), and drummer Joey Castillo (ex-Danzig). The Spread Beaver single "Rocket Dive" soared to No. 4 on the Oricon. Zilch, which was formed in March of that year, had its first album slated for a U.S. release. But on the morning of May 2, 1998, hide was found in his apartment, hung to a doorknob with a towel. That evening, he died. Floods of devastated fans inundated his funeral, with 50,000 gathered at the temple's entrance and 12,000 attending the wake. Over 100 police officers, accompanied by boats and helicopters, monitored the event, which was so catastrophic it made news not only in Asia, but Europe and several major U.S. newspapers, as well. Since then, hide's fan base has swelled to something akin to that of the late Kurt Cobain. In September 1998, his Spread Beaver "Pink Spider" music video won MTV Japan's Viewer's Choice Award. A posthumous album sold madly. LUNA SEA guitarist J and Charlie Clouser of Nine Inch Nails contributed to a Zilch remix album, *BastardEYES*, in 1999, and a museum in hide's honor opened in his hometown, Yokosuka, in 2000.

# Janne Da Arc

MEMBERS Yasu (vocals), You (guitar), Ka-yu (bass), Kiyo (keyboard), Shuji (drums)
EX-MEMBERS Chiba (drums), Ino (bass)
DATES 1991–

After indie hell and finally scoring a major contract, many bands—for one reason or another—break up. Not so with Janne Da Arc. Named after Joan of Arc's appearance in the manga (Japanese graphic novel) *Devilman*, JDA began in 1989 with junior high schoolmates Yasu, Ka-yu, and Kiyo (on vocals, bass, and keyboard, respectively) in Osaka. After a series of lineup shifts and some demo tape experimentation, JDA finally gelled in spring 1996 with guitarist You, who joined in 1991 (it was at that time that the band was named), and drummer Shuji, who joined in 1992 and became official in 1996. That May, it grabbed a spot among other bands at Naniwa Rockets—a popular Osaka club—and in the summer of 1997 released its first official demo tape. Its first solo gig followed in early 1998. But, JDA still didn't have the popularity it wanted. So in April 1998, it adopted a visual look and released two mini-albums, *Dearly* and *Resist*. The elaborate look worked. In 1999, JDA went major, becoming the sole rock band with idol label Avex Trax.

Seven albums later, it's still around and enjoying fresh success. In 2003, concept album *Another Story* was completed, single "Ueta Taiyou" leapt to No. 4 on the Oricon singles chart, and two compilations, *Singles* and *Another Singles*, rose to No. 4 and No. 7, respectively. What stands out undeniably about JDA's music is Kiyo's keyboard, which is always integrated effortlessly into the band's compositions. Catchy and rhythmic, it lends an efficient, multifaceted dimension whatever its sound, synth, strings, or piano. It balances and complements You's blistering guitar work and isn't all stone-set ivory; shared solos with You boast admirable improvisations. Combined, JDA melds to enhance Yasu's singing, coalescing behind his high, youthful vocals like a melodic, driven storm. Since sticking close in the major leagues, JDA has eschewed its visual style—managing to stay hip as rockers, of course—and returned to its original, plot-related roots: in 2003, Yasu wrote a book as a supplement to *Another Story*. The 160-page work, also titled *Another Story*, was described as an "adventure fantasy" and details the story contained within the album's songs. And JDA still attracts new fans, especially since its single "Shining Ray" was used as an ending theme for the anime series *One Piece*. JDA continues to make the same music it always has, creatively, and more of it. Judging by its track record, fans can rest assured that JDA's style and sound—and members—will stay together for a long while.

# Judy And Mary

MEMBERS  Yuki Isoya (vocals), Takuya Asanuma (guitar), Yoshihito Onda (bass), Kohta Igarashi (drums)

DATES  1992–2001

Judy And Mary, the Dr. Jekyll/Mr. Hyde–esque pop-rock band fronted by super-peppy, petite, and playfully petulant vocalist Yuki, was formed in 1992 with Yuki, bassist Onda (who goes by his last name), drummer Kohta, and a support guitarist. After an indie release, it was joined the next year by permanent guitarist Takuya; soon after, thanks to an old demo tape, JAM went major. Its debut single "Power of Love" was released in the fall of 1993, followed by *J.A.M* in January 1994. Two years later, the single "Sobakasu" (Freckles) was used as an opening theme to a popular anime series, *Rurouni Kenshin*, and catapulted the band to big-time fame. JAM appeared on all the major TV music and variety shows, placed eighteenth in the top singles of the year with "Sobakasu," and scored a spot on the Red and White Music Festival. Yuki's piercing, stunningly shrill, helium-fueled vocals are glass-breaking in intensity as well as pitch, and the explosive, daunting star power of her voice is hard to resist—but the boys of Judy And Mary are competent in their own right. Virgin ears might wreck at the get-go, but what compels fans to keep listening is music that both highlights and compliments her singing: deft and complex yet uncrowded and lighthearted, ranging from upbeat to wistful. Together, JAM flips moods and melodies like a monster skateboard, purposefully rowdy, zooming gleefully between tuneful mischief and dementia. Rackety, tangled guitars trail a sense of uncertainty, leaving you eager for the next groove or riff shot to the head. That manic yet solid musical style was Judy And Mary's trademark, and the band didn't give an inch until its breakup in 2001. Decked out in zany, handmade, sometimes avant-garde outfits, JAM always flaunted its makeshift creativeness openly and continued to do so. Eventually, after tinkering with production on 1998's *Pop Life*, Takuya took over for the band's last album, the self-produced *Warp*. JAM champions funny music, and you can take "funny" however you want. With nods to the Chordettes ("Lollipop") and Beatles ("Come Together"), *Warp* plays like a retro ride—but like JAM's other albums, it's sprightly and crazy in a high-flying way to the end. After a side collaboration with jpop singer Chara and Kate Pierson (B-52's) in 1999, Yuki went on to produce two solo albums and four books post-JAM. Takuya reformed his pre-JAM band, Robots, as singer and guitarist.

# Kagrra,

MEMBERS Isshi (vocals), Akiya (guitar), Shin (guitar), Nao (bass), Izumi (drums)
DATES 1998–

Some rock bands draw from current issues and events; others pay tribute to old-school greats. But Kagrra, (spelled with the comma) gets its name and style from almost two centuries ago, basing itself on traditional Japanese culture and history. Composed of vocalist Isshi, guitarists Akiya and Shin, bassist Nao and drummer Izumi, it particularly favors the Heian era (A.D. 794–1185), a time when Chinese, not Japanese, was used in official correspondence, and then by men only. Women were restricted to Japanese—thus, some of the greatest literary works produced in Japanese history, in Japanese, were by women. *Kagura* (the pronunciation of Kagrra,) is an ancient, sacred dance and is written with the meaning "music of god." Kagrra,'s present-day members initially gathered in 1998 under the name CROW. In 2000, CROW changed its name to Kagrra. Kagrra's concept was solid, but its image wasn't to be outdone. Jam-packed among aspiring artists, Kagrra stood out with its decidedly visual dress: elaborate kimono with modern accessories, precious makeup, and convincing cross-dressing. It was as if a troupe of ancient courtesans had traveled through time and plugged into Tokyo's indie scene, cocooned in curtains of fabric and cherry blossom art. Isshi's pan-pipe vocals and the band's bard-like compositions, crossed and weighed with electricity, are elegant, romantic, dissonant works that pull with old fashions and surprise with modern twists: a synth groove here, ribbons of electric guitar there, underscored by hard-hitting drums. There's a melancholic lilt to its music, which carries exotic, non-standard melodies and lines. Simultaneously, it is dramatic, retaining an edginess borne of years underground. Kagrra released a flutter of mini-albums before making its major debut in 2004 with the single "Urei" (Grief), and changing its name once again, adding the comma to reflect the foray. Influenced by such works as poetess Shikibu Murasaki's *The Tale of Genji*, Isshi occasionally writes lyrics in Old Japanese, in a feminine voice, and assumes characters, recreates stories, and bases work on events from the Heian period, particularly on Kagrra,'s first full-length album, *Miyako*. If Kagrra,'s music is not that of god, it certainly is of history. Even the artwork in its packaging embodies the group's unique concept: strikingly clean, bold, anime-style illustrations of kimono-clad women, modern renditions of what once was. From its CD cover art to its dress and its music, in a fast-paced, minute-ticking music business, Kagrra, keeps an old, old history alive.

# Kuroyume

| | |
|---|---|
| MEMBERS | Kiyoharu (vocals), Hitoki (bass) |
| SUPPORTING MEMBERS | Taketomo Sakashita (guitar), Eiji Mitsuzono (drums) |
| EX-MEMBER | Shin (guitar) |
| DATES | 1991–1999 |

The dramatic, elegant goth group Kuroyume ("black dream"), formed in 1991 by Garnet bandmates Kiyoharu and bassist Hitoki with rival guitarist Shin, began its descent upon the Japanese rock scene swathed in head-to-toe black, pale-faced and darkly eye-lined. It produced two albums, *Ikiteita Chuuzetsuji* (Aborted Living Fetus) and *Nakigara wo...* (Corpse...), perching atop the indie charts with its darkly nostalgic style before turning major in 1994. After the 1994 release of mini-album *Cruel*, Shin left. Kiyoharu and Hitoki carried on, but as Shin had done most of the composing, Kuroyume shifted musically—and visually. Gone were the black cloaks, heavy makeup, and haunted sound; in came color and biting experimentation. *Fake Star–I'm Just A Japanese Fake Rocker–* (1996) boasted noisy, electronic synth work; subsequent albums marked detours into concentrated punk and guitar-laden, wickedly obnoxious rock. The band's wardrobe went through similar transformations, comprising every look from light, dressy glam to shirtless, careless grunge. Whatever its style, Kuroyume's work is hugely emotional, each song a vivid sequence in itself. *Corkscrew*'s "Maria" has Kiyoharu's vocals spilling over ska-punk and sparse guitars like jagged syrup. Fan favorite "Like @ Angel," off of *Drug Treatment*, is chest-pounding, relentless, almost menacing. There's rowdy, upbeat, momentum-punched "Spray." And then there are gems on *Fake Star* like "Beams," which shines and suspends sweetly, and "Pistol," cycling with raunchy guitar before breaking into fantastic, brilliant synth. Kiyoharu's vocals are another Kuroyume signature, ranging from roughly hoarse, wired and expressive to tender, hushed, and bittersweet. His singing, peppered with throwaway, quirky flips—as if his vocal chords were tossing their hair—trembles, quavering, with fast vibrato on the upside. Kuroyume attracted more fans as it expanded. (Starting with *Fake Star*, all of its albums went platinum.) But in January 1999, Kiyoharu and Hitoki announced their disbandment, playing their last live at the end of the month. Post-breakup, Hitoki formed a new band, Piranhaheads, while Kiyoharu went on to found SADS and his own record label, FullFace. And Kuroyume faded back whence it had come, leaving only memorable flashbacks of waking melodies.

# La'cryma Christi

MEMBERS    Taka (vocals), Hiro (guitar), Koji (guitar), Shuse (bass), Levin (drums)
DATES      1994–

One has to wonder if La'cryma Christi ever saw its career coming. Besides having a direct line to The Man Upstairs (its name means "tears of Christ"), its lyrics are inspired by art books, astrology, prophecy, and vocalist Taka's own dreams. Initially known as Strippe-D Lady, the band was renamed by Taka after bassist Shuse joined in October 1994, to reflect its new lineup and musical style. While still an indie band, La'cryma had a few strokes of success that fated it for major fame. It sold out its first live show in October 1995 at home in Osaka, followed by a solo stint at Tokyo club Meguro Rock May Kan that winter. Debut single "Siam's Eye" completely sold out; so did mini-album *Warm Snow*. Two tours later, the single "Forest" was released in March 1997 and used as the theme song to a TV series, *Otenki Oneesan* (Weather Girl). The following month, the music video for "Glass Castle"—which had been filmed in Italy—was released. La'cryma went major in May 1997 with its debut single "Ivory Trees"; next came a totally packed, twelve-stop tour. That November, its first major album, *Sculpture of Time*, was released, placing No. 8 on the Oricon chart. Another, shorter tour also sold out that December, and the following year single "Mirai Kouro" (Future Course) plowed to No. 3 on the charts. Taka has a winsome, vibrato-infused voice a la Rush's Geddy Lee—with less helium. Delightfully effortless and easygoing, it is sonorous and spirited, with a thrown-back, aw-shucks aspect that's practically coy. In turn, La'cryma's songs include confident grooves, steady yet sprightly, and embellished with Hiro and Koji's kindred guitars; slow, sweet rock waltzes are held down by Levin's solid, daunting drums. When lighthearted, it's fantastic; when somber, it's forbidding, almost doomful, as if predicting some occult, arcane catastrophe. La'cryma's look was eye-catching, too. Strippe-D Lady had been a very visual act, and until 2000, Hiro's silken, waist-length sheen of shiny black hair was the envy and enchantment of rivals and fans, men and women alike. Since then, the band has toned down to being simply fashionable, preferring leather to lipstick. To boot, La'cryma is well connected. Levin befriended and was guided by the late drummer Randy Castillo (ex-Ozzy Osbourne, Mötley Crüe), and the band was aided, influenced, and mentored by established rockers LUNA SEA. Its other industry pals include Gackt from his Malice Mizer days, Aiji and Jun of PIERROT, and Janne Da Arc's Yasu. Maybe it's no mystery as to how and why La'cryma Christi has stuck around. But its supernaturally inspired (and unnaturally groovy) work will always stand as the epitome of mystic rock.

# L'Arc~en~Ciel

| | |
|---|---|
| MEMBERS | hyde (vocals), ken (guitar), tetsu (bass), yukihiro (drums) |
| EX-MEMBERS | hiro (guitar), pero (drums), sakura (drums) |
| DATES | 1991– |

There is something windy and wistful about L'Arc~en~Ciel, whose name means "the rainbow." Formed by bassist tetsu (who named the band after a French film) with vocalist hyde in Osaka in 1991, L'Arc's initial lineup also included guitarist hiro and drummer pero, but they left the next year. Tetsu convinced his childhood friend, ken, to drop college and play guitar; pero was replaced by another drummer, sakura. L'Arc's first album, *DUNE*, topped the indie charts in April 1993 and got the band a major record deal. Its third album, *heavenly*, flew to No. 3 on the major charts in 1995; *True* debuted at No. 2 in December 1996, rose to No. 1 in January, and clung to the charts for two more months. It seemed L'Arc was sky-bound, but sakura then quit that November. Shocked, L'Arc faded from the scene. But its fans did not. Despite the lull, L'Arc sold out an impending Tokyo Dome concert (56,000 tickets) in a record four minutes. Veteran drummer yukihiro was recruited to record new single "Niji" (Rainbow) and album *HEART*; after a warm welcome at the Dome, he officially joined in January 1998. In 1999, the simultaneous release of *ark* and *ray* flew to No. 1 and No. 2, respectively, setting a record. L'Arc's following continued to grow, and in appreciation, the band asked fans to make an album. In 2001, 100 million fans across Asia eagerly voted to compose the lineup of L'Arc's first compilation, *Clicked Singles Best 13*. (A new song, "Anemone," was added as well.) L'Arc's popularity is no mystery. Hyde's long-reaching, expressive vocals switch easily between falsetto and regular singing; ken's luminous guitar, tetsu's flying, momentum-filled bass lines, and a certain pliant, vibrant, and airy complexity are all L'Arc trademarks. Even at their heaviest, L'Arc's compositions breathe, and the group's ability to change shades without losing form has kept longtime fans and attracted legions of new ones. *HEART*'s "winter fall" is fluid, sentimental pop rock, laced with chimes, strings, and brass; on *ark*, artfully layered "Larva" electronically grooves before metamorphosing into dark, foreboding "Butterfly's Sleep." And spacey-smooth "Neo Universe," off 2000's *REAL* album, positively glides. In 2001, L'Arc again fell silent (and fans cried disbandment) as its members pursued solo projects. But it reappeared in 2003 and once more was successful—this time, internationally. Single "Ready Steady Go" entered the charts at No. 1; its thirteenth album, *SMILE*, floated to No. 2 and was released in North America. All its anime credits in Japan, too, came to fruition, as U.S. fans of series such as *Rurouni Kenshin*, *DNA²*, and *Great Teacher Onizuka* discovered L'Arc's years of work. Finally, a 2004 performance in conjunction with Baltimore's Otakon, the second-largest anime and East Asian culture convention in the United States, made L'Arc the first Japanese rock band to play a major American venue. Now that L'Arc~en~Ciel has stretched across oceans, one question remains: how long will it stay around? For years, it has breezily delighted everywhere it's gone, leaving pots of gold in its wake.

# LOVE PSYCHEDELICO

MEMBERS   Kumi (vocals, guitar), Naoki Sato (guitar, bass, keyboard)
DATES   1997–

The sure guitar of Naoki Sato and steely voice of Kumi joined at the music
club of a top-tier Tokyo university in

1997, forming LOVE PSYCHEDELICO. After storming college radio with a demo tape and releasing an indie cassette (that sold out despite its old-school format), the duo rolled into the major scene in 2000 with debut single "Lady Madonna~yuutsu naru spider~"(Lady Madonna~melancholy spider~), a twangy, slightly trippy number boasting both DELICO's general mood and Kumi's particular range and ease with English. Its debut album, playfully titled *THE GREATEST HITS*, features "Lady Madonna" as its first song and entered the charts at No. 1 in January 2001, staying in the top five for five weeks. DELICO then performed at the South by Southwest music festival in Austin, Texas before whipping around New York, Chicago, Seattle, Los Angeles, and San Francisco that March. It picked up positive press along the way and in July received exposure in the UK. The work paid off: Second album *LOVE PSYCHEDELIC ORCHESTRA* also shot to No. 1, selling over 900,000 copies—and *GREATEST HITS* went double platinum. DELICO's songs are moody, mellow rock gems influenced by the Beatles, Rolling Stones, and Led Zeppelin, with a dab of swank electronica to taste. Its guitars express effortlessly, quavering like summer heat rising off skin in "I mean love me," and reflecting stars on a sand-scratched windshield in "Moonly." Sleek chord changes slide—no, *swing*—together like swiveling hips, and Kumi's voice climbs from husky drawls to no-nonsense demands with all the bittersweet indignation of Gloria Gaynor. Thanks to its versatile yet unique sound, DELICO's music continues to spread in Japan and elsewhere. Third album *LOVE PSYCHEDELICO III* claimed No. 2 on the charts, lingering in the top ten for nearly a month, and the pair kicked off a new rock festival, the two-day Rock Odyssey featuring Aerosmith and the Who, in 2004. Its high quality, modern twist tributes will make you groove like the wild-sultry thing you are. LOVE PSYCHEDELICO is all about being free: As Kumi sings in "waltz," free as the sky.

# LUNA SEA

MEMBERS  Ryuichi (vocals), Sugizo (guitar), Inoran (guitar), J (bass), Shinya (drums)
DATES  1986–2000

There are bands that feel your pain, and then there are bands that play it for you. LUNA SEA did both. Inoran and J founded the band in 1986 as Lunacy before Ryuichi, Sugizo, and Shinya joined in 1989. It then released a three-song demo tape, "Lunacy," and changed its name to LUNA SEA in 1990. Indie LUNA SEA sold out club after club, and was scouted and signed to indie label Extasy Records a year later. After releasing its self-titled, full-length debut, LUNA SEA went major with 1992's *Image*, which entered the charts at No. 9. It scored its first No. 1 single in the autumn of 1994 with "True Blue"; its following album, *Mother*, reached No. 3. Then, in the winter of 1995, LUNA SEA sold out Tokyo Dome. In 1996 and 1998, respectively, albums *Style* and *Shine* took over the charts at No. 1. LUNA SEA's music moves quickly but intelligibly, with a darkly frenetic, creative energy. An inherent hollow darkness pervades nearly all of its music: the opening of *Mother*, "Loveless," is lyrical, fluidly tender, with restless drums and a pulling undertow bass. Ryuichi's frustrated vocals range from emphatic wailing to being stylish and smooth, hushed like black silk. Shinya's churning drums splash and crash on the title track of *Shine*, which begs in its bright rarity to be used as a synchronized swimming number. Angst-filled vocals, churning, mournful, pessimistic guitars, stomach-socking drums—it all makes you want to hurt for more. Like its mentor and predecessor, X, early LUNA SEA was visual with teased hair, pale makeup, and plenty of eyeliner; however, it cultivated its own look, a monochromatic one not nearly as flamboyant. By 1994, everyone's hair was down (some bleached, but down nonetheless). Musically, LUNA SEA was more goth rock than speed metal with Ryuichi as a thicker, dark mouthpiece. After the band took time off to pursue solo work in 1997, he was like a panther with syrupy vocals, having made a foray as a singer of love songs. It was that gradual but evident evolution that led to LUNA SEA's disbandment. (Its last single, "Love Song," though a deftly constructed, sweetly crooning farewell, is a complete 180 from anything that could have come out of the group a decade earlier.) In 2000, the band chose to break up upon consensus that future albums could only be a letdown when compared with its last album, *Lunacy*. Judging from the title it would seem that LUNA SEA's members had completed a linear story amid a maddening, loveless world.

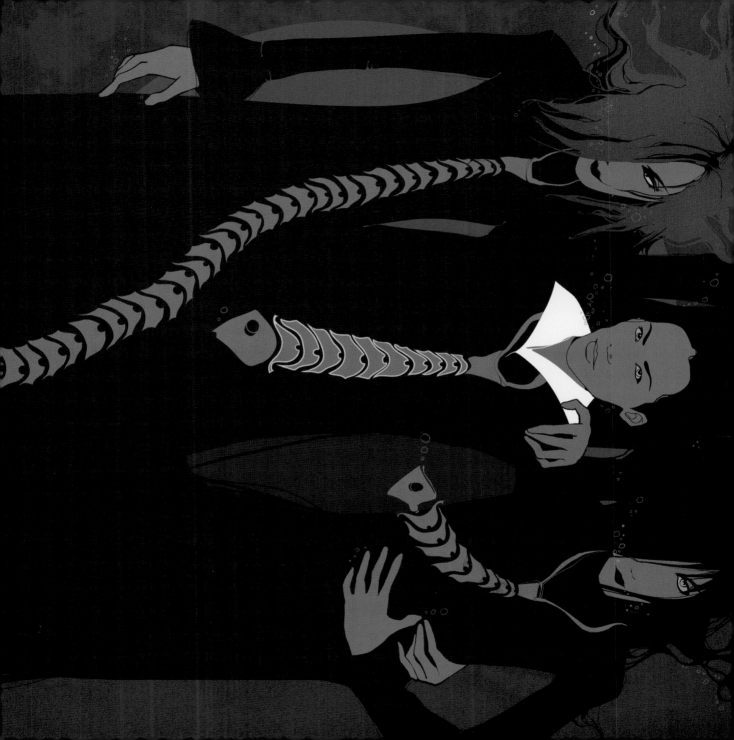

# Malice Mizer

MEMBERS     Klaha (vocals), Mana (guitar, synth), Közi (guitar, synth), Yu~ki (bass)
EX-MEMBERS    Gaz (drums), Tetsu (vocals), Gackt (vocals), Kami (drums)
DATES      1992–2001

Clad in elaborate, gender-bending make-up and costumes fit for vampiric royalty, Malice Mizer was one group that stood out in the scrambled wave (dubbed "new visual" by the Japanese media) that swept the Japanese rock scene in the 1990s. Its concept was based on the question of human nature, which it defined as "malicious misery"; hence, the abbreviated Malice Mizer. Ranking among the most fantastic transvestites of them all, guitarist Mana is the epitome of dramatic and theatrical, a mute, elegant Victorian doll with an electric guitar. Thanks to his fascination with classical music and Italian horror films, vast oceans of synth met not only rock guitar, but piano, organ, accordion, and strings, creating a juxtaposition simultaneously fatalistic and beautiful. Malice Mizer's histrionics struck a chord with its audiences. After vocalist Gackt ascended the throne in the fall of 1995 (former singer Tetsu left at the end of 1994), second album *Voyage–sans retour–* debuted at No. 1 on the indie charts, and a summer tour in 1997 sold out completely. Its major debut, *merveilles*, grasped No. 2 on the album charts in 1998. That spring Malice Mizer sold out Nippon Budokan in two minutes. Church bells, twisted waltzes — an intrinsic melancholy permeates Malice Mizer's music. It stops and starts like an ill-fated carriage hitting rocks in the road. It swirls circuitously into a circus nightmare. It halts, off-kilter, a carnival spectacle peppered with techno-trance whiplash. Mana and Kozi's thin, twin guitars are sinister, lethal and wicked sometimes, luminous and nebulous at others. Classical references are blatant: a slice of "Madrigal" is a direct, modulated lift of Mozart's "Turkish March"; "Bois de merveilles" is très Shostakovich. For *Voyage* and *merveilles*, Gackt's molasses voice smoothed everything over, but he abdicated to start a solo career at the start of 1999. Then, it was as if Malice Mizer's concept caught hold of its members. In the summer of 1999, drummer Kami died unexpectedly of a brain hemorrhage. The following album *Bara no Seidou* (Rose Sanctuary) read like an entire requiem on CD with a chorus that would make Karl Orff proud. The band tried to continue with backup vocalist Klaha (who sang on *Bara*) but officially disbanded in December 2001. Gutarist Közi embarked on a solo career. Mana, after continuing with visual groups Schwarz Stein and Moi dix Mois, launched an international campaign, opening his Mon Amour fan club to fans overseas.

# Miyavi

vocals, guitar

DATES 2002–

He's always stood out. At seventeen, guitarist and backup screamer Miyabi was the youngest member of visual indie band Dué le quartz when he joined in 1999. When Dué disbanded in September 2002, some fans found solace: Miyabi was continuing activity, solo, under the name Miyavi. But when Miyavi struck out on his own, it was a doozy for Dué fans expecting things to stay the same. Miyavi is unique—according to a tattoo written in Japanese on his right arm, he's "The one and only/In heaven and on earth"—and he cultivated his own personal style. Gone were the kimono, flamboyant cross-dressing, and androgynous makeup, black vinyl, and rhinestone crown. Miyavi fortified his upper body with an arsenal of tattoos and piercings. And his music was different, too. Peppered with versatile guitarwork, Miyavi's music alternately stings and gyrates. On his second solo album, 2003's *Galyuu,* thick curtains of staticky, metallic electronic-industrial noise cascade across tracks. "Ashita, tenki ni naare" (I hope tomorrow will be sunny) is a head-grooving number with acoustic guitar. Another song is like something from the Violent Femmes. Guitars are wielded both rhythmically and melodically. And like his guitars, Miyavi's vocals are varied. He's got a grip on scream-singing and nasty, hoarse, purposeful gurgling; unplugged songs give way to deadpan, smoky singing. He can be loud and screamy or cool, raw-throated, and melodic. And then there's this gruff hemming and hawing thing he does that's, well, kind of sexy. For fans, what's even sexier is that Miyavi takes time to interact. He reads fan mail at live shows and posts messages (as much as seven times a day) on his Web site on everything from cigarettes (he's trying to quit) to salmon (he once ate it three meals in a row—smoked, grilled, and raw). Because his popularity swelled in Japan, he was in enough demand to be slated for a clutch of U.S. anime and Japanese culture conventions in 2003, sending fans and would-be fans into online convulsions. Miyavi didn't come to the States—a staff member had misscheduled—but high hopes hang that he will in the future. This clucking, mumbling, quacking, loopy, howling, cooing rattling upstart full of artful, myriad clamor seems out of control. Yet, he remains focused. At twenty-three, Miyavi hit the big time, making his major debut, "rokku no gyakushuu~suupaa sutaa no jouken~" (rock counterattack~super star demands~), in October 2004. He might be weird, but for a rock scene that's only getting older, he could be, as his tattoo reads, The One.

# Mr. Children

MEMBERS  Kazutoshi Sakurai (vocals, guitar), Kenichi Tahara (guitar), Keisuke Nakagawa (bass), Hideya Suzuki (drums)

DATES  1989–

Its name may sound villainous, but Mr. Children is more realistic than evil. It began as three-piece high school band with singer-songwriter Kazutoshi Sakurai, guitarist Kenichi Tahara, and bassist Keisuke Nakagawa in 1985. Two years after drummer Hideya Suzuki joined in 1987, it proclaimed itself Mr. Children in 1989, graduated in 1990, and was scouted in 1991. It signed to the just-established Toy's Factory label, and with 1992's *Everything*, began releasing music to decent sales. Long-lasting success takes time, and it wasn't until 1994 that Mr. Children found itself in the spotlight. That summer, its single "innocent world" won the Nihon Record Taisho Grand Prize and twice touched No. 1 on the charts; another single, "Cross road," was used as the theme to a TV series and became Mr. Children's first platinum seller. Fourth album *Atomic Heart*—which included both songs—went double platinum after its release in September. By 1995, it had embarked on a doubleheader tour, playing Nippon Budokan multiple times. A documentary movie of the tours followed, the theme song for which stayed at No. 1 for two weeks. "Cross road" was widely popular, but it branded Mr. Children as a love song band. "innocent world" marked the band's change in style from popular love songs to more introverted works. Sakurai entered an introspective period, and the band spent four months in New York, recording *Shinkai* (Deep Sea) with Lenny Kravitz engineer Henry Hirsch. Love existed alongside despair and other painful emotions on *Shinkai*—and it went triple platinum, despite its reality. That same duality appeared in the name of Mr. Children's post-album tour, called "regress or progress." It was a dark period; still, the band played Tokyo Dome in 1997. And then it went on break. Mr. Children's style ranges from simple, folksy, and low-key to complex and digitally enhanced. On *Atomic Heart*, supergroovy "Love Connection" smacks of the Rolling Stones, additionally sprouting bass and funky wa-wa guitar; "Dance Dance Dance," punctuated with infectious samples of scrambled guitar and harmonized backup vocals, and spattered with steely drums, will make you instantly footloose. But *Shinkai* track "Hana–Mémento Mori–"(Flower–Mémento Mori–) is somber in comparison, lilting and lamenting with a singalong, sadly tender chorus. In 1999, the comeback album *Discovery* went straight to No. 1 on the charts, renewing, well, everything. Three albums and a fistful of No. 1 singles later, Mr. Children shows no sign of slowing down. It appeared in 2003 as the happy ending on a nationally televised New Year's Eve musical marathon after groups younger (Gackt), shinier (Ayumi Hamasaki), and smoother (Chemistry). And perhaps that's simply because Mr. Children has been around for so long and gone through so much. Its songs soothe with tunefulness and energy—but perhaps the most comforting thing is knowing that what's behind them is hardly candy-coated.

# Penicillin

MEMBERS   Hakuei (vocals), Chisato (guitar), Gisho (bass), O-Jiro (drums)
DATES   1992–

Take Penicillin to remember what guitar solos are. Formed in 1992 by high
school friends Hakuei, Chisato, Gisho,
and O-Jiro, this guitar-heavy band of
would-be experimental misfits packed
small-time clubs before producing a
mini-album, indie debut *Penicillin Shock,*
in 1994. Its first full-length album, *Missing Link*, was released later that year to underground acclaim; two years later, Penicillin infiltrated the major scene with its single
"Blue Moon" and another album, *Vibe*. After dabbling in side projects, the fivesome
followed up with 1997's *Limelight*. Penicillin's styles vary between albums, straddling
L.A. rock influences, a dissonance characteristic of the Japanese indie scene, and
its own segmented, explorative streak. Old-school guitar anthems glitter, ricochet,
and sparkle courtesy of Chisato, whose tight, sparse, and raw playing interspersed
with glossy, ornamental flourishes creates an effect both elegant and flamboyant.
Hakuei's breathy, hollow vocals float above and burrow in, at times echoing from
below. They warble and tremble, squeaky-edged, sounding like anywhere from Kuro-
yume-era Kiyoharu (*Limelight*) to Dir en grey's Kyo (*Union Jap*). Mix in some industrial drum synth fancywork together with O-Jiro's hard, sticky drums. Penicillin's music
may seem disconnected and incongruous, with little continuity between albums.
Put simply, it's experimental. But there's always Hakuei's emphatic, husky, airy
vocals and Chisato's finesse-with-balls guitar to keep you in line. Penicillin's look
was also initially extreme and dramatic. Tall, svelte Hakuei easily doubled as a strikingly beautiful woman, appearing in everything from long, blond curls and dresses
to skin-tight leather and scandalously short shorts. Dark-haired, dashing Gisho
complemented him, playing prince to Hakuei's mademoiselle. Chisato and O-Jiro
made themselves up in suits. Though its effect may have changed, it seems Penicillin
has yet to wear off. Thanks to its consistently deliberate evolution and history, it has
enjoyed gradually growing success. (*Missing Link* was such an indie jewel, it was re-
released twice.) And as Penicillin's fanbase expanded, the band responded in kind
by becoming one of the first Japanese rock groups to open its fan club, Quarter Doll,
to international members in 1998. After breaking again in 1999, Penicillin performed
a nationally televised duet with Bon Jovi in 2000, and it has released an album
each year since. And that's a good thing. Because to ward off the blues, sometimes
you need an ex-supermodel to inject good, old-fashioned guitar riffs into your head.

# PIERROT

MEMBERS Kirito (vocals), Aiji (guitar), Jun (guitar), Kohta (bass), Takeo (drums)
EX-MEMBERS Hidelow (vocals), Luka (drums)
DATES 1994–

Call PIERROT if you need a dictatorship. Ice-cold, charismatic leader Kirito rules not only with a gloved fist, but with dagger-eye makeup and scores of black tattoos. He's nepotistic (younger brother Kohta is PIERROT's bassist), and when he's not onstage commanding throngs of Followers (that's PIERROT's fan club), he's out talking on the radio and writing musical propaganda. PIERROT was formed in Nagano with guitarist Jun, then-guitarist Kirito, and Kohta in 1994. After its indie debut and a 1995 shuffle that brought in drummer Takeo, guitarist Aiji, and placed Kirito on vocals, its second album, *Pandora no Hako* (Pandora's Box), sold out in the wake of its concerts in 1996. In 1998 and 1999, a fistful of top ten singles marked PIERROT's big-time assault. The group's live charisma keeps PIERROT in power. Whole floors of fans mimic Kirito's gestures onstage, and in April 1999 the band sold out Nippon Budokan. PIERROT's first live video, final footage of its *RISING A [MAD SKY]* tour, shot to No. 1 on the Oricon that September. The next day, it sold out Yokohama Arena. By 2000, PIERROT had toured Japan nine times over. PIERROT's signature sound includes Kirito's high, static-infused vocals and the motor power from Jun and Aiji's twin guitars. Jun's synth guitar and Kohta's bass form an undertow combination ordered by Takeo's hard-hitting drums, which offsets both Aiji and Kirito in its thickness. Elegant flashes of laser and bottle-rocket guitar zip and soar in "Dramatic Neo Anniversary"; "Home Sick" has luminous touch-type guitar. And then there are seemingly sweet, optimistic ballads like "Birthday" and "Cocoon." After switching record labels in 2000, PIERROT went on to produce some of its finest work, and its more recent albums have been chasing its live video rankings. 2002's *Heaven~The Customized Landscape~* debuted at No. 7 on the charts; 2003's *ID ATTACK* exploded at No. 3. Both albums are laced with dissonance, a touch of vocal distortion, and shades of electronica, with a dash of irony and a pinch of cynicism. They hover somewhere between intricate and detailed, sophisticated yet danceable, without losing the uniqueness of the members' ensemble. Conceptually, PIERROT is darkly sardonic and biologically themed, metallic and imminent; it holds civilization in contempt. A prickly, shiny sheen finishes all its work, giving it the sound and feel of a thousand silver needles. Likewise, Kirito can be caustically, enviably witty, sarcastic, and intelligent. But for all its disdain for the status quo, PIERROT does what it has to. It's a totalitarian regime worth joining.

# the pillows

MEMBERS — Sawao Yamanaka (vocals, guitar), Yoshiaki Manabe (guitar), Shinichiro Sato (drums)
SUPPORTING MEMBERS — Tatsuya Kashima (bass, 1992–99), Jun Suzuki (bass, 1999–)
EX-MEMBER — Kenji Ueda (bass)
DATES — 1989–

In the Japanese animation series *Fooly Cooly* (*FLCL*), a twelve-year-old boy gets plowed by a Vespa and clocked in the head with the bass guitar by its rider—a pink-haired girl. The same gunning, guitar-wielding girl later runs over his dad, shows up for tea at his house, and guess what? She's the new house-maid. That zany, offbeat aspect drives the series, and it's what drives the soundtrack, too—a soundtrack done by the pillows, a trio of equally energe-tic, neurotic rockers. Formed in 1989 by Sawao Yamanaka, Yoshiaki Manabe, Shinichiro Sato, and Kenji Ueda, the pillows made their major debut in 1991 with the album *Moon Gold*, but in 1992, Ueda left to start his own record label. Activity faltered, but in 1994 the pillows regrouped and switched labels. The remaining members have been grooving ever since, sporting support bassists as they see fit. Five years later, animation studio Gainax scooped up three pillows albums, *Little Busters, Runners High,* and *Happy Bivouac*—and the pillows also composed two singles specifically—for *FLCL*. Sweet, artful melodies and rowdy, mischievous guitar embody the pil-lows' music, which spans low-key good-naturedness and full-throttle punky-spunk. Reggae and folk rock influences surface, but there's also nothing like some motor guitar juxtaposed with mini bleats to get fans going—and cause a crazed need to jump, jump-kick, and crowd-surf. The pillows also tout laid-back, easygoing numbers that simply coast. Effectively stamped by Yamanaka's slightly nasal but clear-cutting, throaty vocals, their versatile sound is one of sun, guts, and gas. The pillows remained relatively obscure in Japan, but in 2002, *FLCL* was released in the United States and was broadcast on Cartoon Net-work's Adult Swim in 2003. Throngs of viewers were endeared to the group's music, which can now be heard at anime conventions and elsewhere. On the side, Yamanaka heads his own record company, Delicious Label, and Manabe dips with his reggae group, Nine Miles. Ever since 2003, the pil-lows have been on the up and up, and it's no wonder. As a match for any-thing super-charged, comically off-kilter yet sensitive, they're an ideal choice.

# Princess Princess

MEMBERS  Kaori Okui (vocals, guitar), Kanako Nakayama (guitar), Atsuko Watanabe (bass),
Tomoko Konno (keyboard), Kyoko Tomita (drums)

DATES  1983–1996

Take a strong-willed, bombastic, vivacious, and bright teenaged girl with talent, originality, skills, and savvy. Multiply by five. Make them Japanese, and you've got Princess Princess. Formed in 1983 when its members—vocalist and chief composer Kaori Okui, guitarist Kanako Nakayama, bass player Atsuko Watanabe, keyboardist Tomoko Konno, and drummer Kyoko Tomita—were as young as sixteen, PriPri (as it's nicknamed) was a girls-only group that would be novel anywhere, but especially in a country whose most popular musical acts were routinely pre-packaged, manufactured, even manipulated, and a rock scene crammed with men. It started small. PriPri wrote just one song on its first release, 1986's

Kiss De Crime, but its full-length debut, 1987's *TELEPORTATION*, had all songs but one self-made. A single, "Sekai De Ichiban Atsui Natsu" (The Hottest Summer In The World), was released that year, but it took two more before PriPri broke through completely. In May 1989, the single "Diamonds" debuted at No. 2 on the charts, stealing No. 1 twice and staying in the top ten for four months. At the same time, a remix of "Sekai" debuted at No. 1 that July and stayed in the top five for two months. The following year, PriPri's fifth album, "*LOVERS*," debuted at No. 4. A skilled, energetic sound and semi-cheesy yet creative and infectious image was what got PriPri so far. It touted teased and feathered hair, big hats and stretch pants, belts and bangles, and kitschy, super self-coordinated outfits, performing in everything from hot pink, barely-there mini-dresses, to blouses, boots, and thigh-high leggings. A year before the visual band X went major, Nakayama and Watanabe were like hide and Taiji in rags and glam coats—without the heavy makeup. Unlike punk-influenced Shonen Knife, PriPri's big style resembles that of '80s hair bands—Van Halen, Bon Jovi, and a few bands in between. Full of spidery synth and badass guitar solos, its fresh, energetic music ranges from sweet, gentle numbers to wicked, foreboding, and even dramatic ones. Husky, fast-warbling songbird Okui's enthusiastic vocals span well over an octave, flying and dipping within catchy, short phrases. A touch of lyricism tops it all off. In 1996, PriPri disbanded, citing musical differences. An official statement would have been customary, but PriPri's members instead embarked on a final, nationwide tour to explain itself to its fans and the reason for its breakup. (That's real royalty.) And if you think its audience was all girls agog, think again. Plenty of guys pumped their fists (albeit ironically) to "Go Away Boy." At a time when rock was hardly being taken seriously, let alone women in rock, PriPri stage-jumped its way through the nascent scene and made its own decisions. It was its own entity and represented a huge leap forward in the Japanese music industry, fun yet formidable. Its like has not been seen since.

# Psycho le Cému

MEMBERS  Daishi (vocals), Aya (guitar), Lida (guitar), Seek (bass), Yura (drums)
DATES  1999–

It's a bird! It's a plane! It's Psycho le Cému. Notorious for its getups, Psycho le Cému (say psycho-le-SHEM, PLC for short) came flying out of Osaka in 1999, and it's been hard for devoted fans not to shell out a buck or two since—for costume materials, anyway. PLC is a superhero band—comic book visual kei—and its members are each a cosplay challenge. Oh, and they play instruments, too. Vocalist Daishi, guitarists Aya and Lida, bassist Seek, and drummer Yura marked PLC's major debut in 2001 with the single "Ai no Uta," grabbing No. 6 on the charts. But let's get back to their costumes. PLC's members dress to impress, and because of their extreme outfits, they've been featured as special guests at anime conventions in both Japan and the United States. Between pink-haired, Tinker Bell–esque Aya and furry, ducky (and sometimes tentacle-sprouting) Seek monster, it's hard to be angsty with PLC. And if you didn't think a Japanese man could go platinum blond and look royally Slavic, take a peek at Yura. In 2004, the band's reputation for looking completely different got it billings at two major Stateside conventions: Pacific Media Expo in Anaheim, California, and Project A-Kon in Dallas, Texas. Spectacle sells, but it doesn't hurt to have help. PLC had a hand in the business; it shares its management company with established rockers PIERROT and La'cryma Christi. Its producer, Masahide Sakuma, has worked with the likes of Judy And Mary, Kuroyume, and GLAY. And in 2004, it began to collaborate with industry pillars THE ALFEE. Its cheesy, repetitive, techno-electrolyzed music, though detailed, isn't quite as substantial as its uniforms—it's a busy mix of darker, more cynical bands and weird, circus-loopy telephone electronica. Compared to other singers, Daishi's vocals are blown-out, less persuasive. But PLC still has room to grow. It's entertaining, if not entirely eye candy. It's springtime visual kei, bright and impish—cross-dressing included, angst, blood, and chains sold separately—unless you piss off Seek. It may leave something to be desired musically, but at least it's got style and team spirit.

# Sheena Ringo

SUPPORTING MEMBERS  vocals, guitar, piano, drums
DATES  various
1998–2004

Sexy without being slutty, violent yet thoughtful, solo artist Sheena Ringo knew how to lose control with style. Sudden, shocking, spooky, yet sweet—over six years solo, the avid avant-garde artist has proven with a trio of albums that she's hardly a saccharine, bubblegum-popping, doe-eyed icon. If there was anything to worship about Sheena Ringo, it's her dark, creative innovation, her discomforting ability, her unabashed flouting of convention. A national music festival win and other music awards delivered Ringo to the major stage in 1998, and she didn't disappoint. Debut album *Muzai Moratorium* sold over a million copies; second album *Shoso Strip* overshot 2 million. But what really mattered was that all that success placed the production reins within Ringo's grasp: third album *Karuki Zamen Kuri no Hana* (Chlorine, Semen, Chestnut Flower) became the first work she produced entirely on her own, with all the resources and artistic direction she could ever want. Moving against the idol-crowded scene in Japan was risky, but *KZK* sold nearly half a million copies, proving even the most conservative market could be provoked by an unusual young woman's creative, bar-breaking vision. Ringo's haunting, challenging songs push limits that are musical, visual, emotional, cultural, and poetic. Her warbling, warning voice, which starkly contrasts with her twisted mess of electric guitar and electronica, ranges anywhere from a harsh croon, a touch demonic and demented, to loud, boisterous, wrathful rockette howling, and beyond to nostalgic. She blends traditional Japanese elements in a bizarre but successful fashion: Imagine a female, kimono-clad attendant taking a smoke break, a geisha slamming on an electric guitar, or a koto performer flipping the bird.

With all the abstractions, there is always something to ground you. Ringo's look was unsettling, but she had a natural, trademark mole. Her music careens and wails, but it's built on a blues-rock foundation. Ringo's lyrics, too, are frank and deliberate, and her music videos aren't about sunshine and flowers, nor are they belly-baring. After the release of a new single and her 2003 tour, Ringo announced the end of her solo career, had her mole cosmetically removed, and joined her primary backing band, Tokyo Jihen, as its vocalist in 2004. But for artists and musicians everywhere—particularly women in male-dominated surroundings—her insolent and controversial legacy remains.

# SADS

| | |
|---|---|
| MEMBERS | Kiyoharu (vocals), Taketomo Sakashita (guitar), Masaru Kobayashi (bass), Eiji Mitsuzono (drums) |
| EX-MEMBERS | Tetsuhiro Tanuma (bass), Masahiro Muta (drums) |
| DATES | 1999– |

SADS is foreplay. It's sex rock. It's ex-Kuroyume vocalist Kiyoharu with a fistful of ex-Kuroyume tour support musicians, and it got off to a strong start by playing a four-location set in the UK after its formation on April Fool's Day, 1999. Its debut single "TOKYO" shot to No. 2 on the charts that July; in September, its first album, *SAD BLOOD ROCK 'N' ROLL*, clenched No. 3. Follow-up *BABYLON* debuted at No. 1 in 2000. SADS continued to work, and its live performances didn't let fans down. In early 2001, two simultaneously released live videos, "Conclusion of my BABYLON" and "The INTRODUCTION," claimed the No.1 and 2 spots on the charts; even after the band switched drummers and labels, maxi-single "PORNO STAR" and album *THE ROSE GOD GAVE ME* still landed top five spots that summer. Regular radio programs ensued, followed by a thirty-one-stop, thirty-two-concert tour. After playing Nippon Budokan, SADS held its countdown live show at Nagoya Diamond at the end of the year. And perhaps that's because SADS's music is so damn sexy. With song titles like "PORNO STAR," you have to have the balls to back it up. It's swank, swarthy, and smoldering; it's in your face in a dark, subtly glamorous way, with nothing to prove. Kiyoharu's electric crooning crawls under your skin and up your shirt—maybe into your pants if you listen closely. Slow guitar tunes trail like fingers on skin, held down by stifled drums, climaxing in music that undulates easily, grooves and coasts effortlessly. It will keep you transfixed, almost hypnotized—the rock equivalent of a strip show. (If you're curious, Kiyoharu wears glitter and glam to complement his smoky, scratchy, super-choked vocals. Because he's a fashion magnet, too.) In 2002, SADS produced an independent, untitled album before engaging in a nine-month marathon tour—seventy-nine locations and 131 performances—titled "SADS TOUR GOODBYE 2002!! 'BEAUTIFUL DAYS' FOR HEAVY PETTING." Another countdown concert was held at the end of 2002, and it seemed SADS would retire. But in 2003, it released a fifth album, *13*, and the single "Masquerade." Kiyoharu embarked on a solo career and released his first album, *poetry*, in April 2004. But one can only hope that SADS isn't completely spent just yet.

# SEX MACHINEGUNS

MEMBERS
Anchang (vocals, guitar), Circuit V. Panther (guitar), Samurai W. Kenjilaw (bass),
Speed Star Sypan Joe (drums)

EX-MEMBERS
Madpower (drums), Sussy (guitar), Clutch J. Himawari (drums), Noisy (bass)

DATES
1990–

Composed of badass, glammed-out, neurotic troublemakers, SEX MACHINEGUNS (inspired by the Sex Pistols) crashed the Japanese indie scene in 1996, sporting heavy metal with comic lyrics. Formed in 1990 by vocalist Anchang, guitarist Sussy, bassist Noisy, and drummer Madpower, they gained popularity by word of mouth before striking a major deal. After debut single "Hanabi–la Dai Kaiten" (Fireworks–Big Rotation) was released in 1998, SM sold out a nationwide tour and scored a gig at Tokyo's Nippon Budokan in early 2000. They then set off a round of top twenty hits and three albums. In 2001, *Barbe-Q Michael* weighed in at No. 7 on the charts; 2002's *Ignition* started up at No. 8. What's great about SEX MACHINEGUNS is that despite sounding like Slayer and early Metallica, they aren't necessarily angry. It's more like being greeted at a restaurant by Iron Maiden. It's that fun-furious combination that gives SM their reputation.

Anchang's singing is more entertaining than Satanic; harmonized, it can sound Bostonesque (try "Peace of Mind"). His shrill voice suits the band's thrashing, thick style by leaping into spitfire yodels, high and long. Heavy guitars and speedy, fast-flying (sometimes majestic) riffs abound, plowing, shredding, and storming with relentlessly staccato drums. Yet, the band's songs pay tribute to *mikan* (Satsuma oranges) and relate stories of life as a dog, complete with bow-wow screaming. If this sounds doofball, even a little like Spinal Tap, you've hit SM on the head. And maybe all the band needs is a spontaneously combusting drummer to top things off. But jokes aside, it has had its share of problems. Lineup changes have dogged SM's heels. Two years after replacing Madpower in 1997, drummer SSS Joe was sidelined with a back injury. In 2001, the original guitarist, Sussy, bowed out. A best-of album was released in 2002, and in April 2003, the group announced a post-summer tour breakup. In 2004, SEX MACHINEGUNS reformed with new bassist Samurai W. Kenjilaw and the return of SSS Joe; a new single, "Demaido Itchokusen" (Nothing but Home Delivery), was released in November. Only time will tell with this revved-up, funny-gunning band. Can they get it up again?

# SHAZNA

| | |
|---|---|
| MEMBERS | IZAM (vocals), A.O.I (guitar), NIY (bass) |
| EX-MEMBER | Katsura (drums) |
| DATES | 1993–2000 |

In 1997, the trio SHAZNA won the Yuusen Taisho award (Japan's equivalent of a Listener's Choice Award) for Best New Band. Its vocalist, IZAM, was a boy who looked and dressed like a girl. And that's because SHAZNA was considered a "new generation visual band" in Japan, part of the "visual boom" that also included La'cryma Christi and Malice Mizer. SHAZNA began in 1993 when bassist NIY—the older brother of its first bassist, and meaning "older brother" in Japanese—joined IZAM, guitarist A.O.I, and drummer Katsura. As part of its management's roster, it played annual concerts with fellow bands La'cryma Christi and PIERROT. As an indie band, its sound was heavy with thrash guitars, IZAM's vocals hard and hollow. The flatly minimalist style went on until Katsura left after the release of mini-album *Raspberry Time*. A session drummer was hired for *Promise Eve*. Then, SHAZNA's sound began to lighten, diversify, and become unique, culminating in *Gold Sun and Silver Moon*. IZAM is a convincing cross-dresser, androgynously pouty. He's donned dresses, skirts, women's kimono, and dyed his hair (a most becoming magenta). CD packaging has him doing things like eating ice cream and being generally girlish, demure and coquettish, made up, and happily so. (For the record, he is straight.) Though not as questionable gender-wise, A.O.I and NIY hold up their end by looking like rockers. SHAZNA went major in 1997 and debuted with its single "Melty Love," a bittersweet, winsomely catchy number that was remade several times. IZAM had wanted to play music and wear makeup since childhood, influenced deeply by Boy George and the Culture Club. And album debut *Gold Sun and Silver Moon* sounds Culture Club–esque with IZAM's light, lilting vocals and bubbly, pop-techno embellishments flourishing across the rock setup. SHAZNA's last release was a compilation album in 2000, and the band hasn't been heard from since. IZAM went on to pursue various solo projects. Still, SHAZNA's work ultimately exemplifies the lighter side of visual kei—possibly the lightest. It's fizzy, carbonated, and danceable. Somehow, SHAZNA had made the transition from a cheap beer to pretty Perrier.

# SHEENA & THE ROKKETS

MEMBERS  Sheena (vocals), Makoto Ayukawa (guitar), Nobuyuki "Navi" Watanabe (bass),
Kazuhide Kawashima (drums)

DATES  1978–

The story of SHEENA & THE ROKKETS is the stuff from which legends are made. In 1978, guitarist Makoto Ayukawa left home to do the right thing—join a rock band. Sheena left home a week later to do her own thing. The pair met in Tokyo a month later and created SHEENA & THE ROKKETS. After debut single "Namida no Highway" (Highway of Tears) was released in October, SHEENA & THE ROKKETS played their first gig at an all-night rock festival at Kyushu University on November 22, Sheena's birthday. The next day, they opened for Elvis Costello in Osaka. A tour with Costello through Fukuoka and Tokyo followed. They played four nights with the Ramones in the summer of 1980, after Ayukawa had joined the Yellow Magic Orchestra on tour after a guest stint. What's more, their rock fest record is stunning. Not many bands can boast having played any rock festival for 26 straight years (New Year's Rock Fes, 1978–2004); then again, not many possess such an outstanding pair as Ayukawa and Sheena. Ayukawa's soulful, seamless, bluesy guitar and his trademark Costello glasses (sunglasses, now) along with Sheena's Cher–meets–Janis Joplin vocals and her mane of wild, Amazon hair are visual-sonic mavericks. Stripped-down guitars and drums hold down the camp, occasionally boosted with organ, a saxophone, or harmonica. Sometimes Ayukawa sings without losing the funky front, but who knew a Japanese woman could have the stage presence of Tina Turner or sound like Robert Plant? Even on studio recordings, Sheena's screeching, howling intensity will eat you alive. Decades into their career, SHEENA & THE ROKKETS are still in tip-top shape, still gigging between tributes, cover songs, solo projects, and their own original work. The group appeared in New York City in 1988 and played CBGB with the Cowboy Junkies in 1993. They played the White Stage at Fuji Rock Festival 2003 (crowd capacity: 10,000) in a lineup that included Iggy Pop, The Mad Capsule Markets, and Anthrax, Sheena in a sequined mini-dress and black boots with stiletto heels that would make a dominatrix cringe. And when *School of Rock* premiered in Japan, SHEENA & THE ROKKETS were there, sleek as ever. According to the *Japan Times*, the MC asked them how they stayed so trim. Ayukawa's reply: "When you rock every day, you don't have time to get fat."

# Shonen Knife

| | |
|---|---|
| MEMBERS | Naoko Yamano (vocals, guitar, bass, keyboard), Atsuko Yamano (drums, bass, vocals) |
| SUPPORTING MEMBER | Mana (drums) |
| EX-MEMBER | Michie Nakatani (vocals, bass, keyboard) |
| DATES | 1981– |

Long before anime and the Internet spread Japanese music to America, the all-female Japanese rock band Shonen Knife was a breakthrough all by itself. Influenced by the Beatles, Ramones, Kinks, and late '70s punk bands, teenaged sisters Naoko and Atsuko Yamano combined with Michie Nakatani in the early '80s to form an old-school, toned-down, back-to-basics band named after a brand of pencil sharpening knife. The cute-dangerous combo (*shonen* means "boy" in Japanese) stuck. The group may not look like rock animals, but Shonen Knife's outwardly innocent, good-girl demeanor belies its prowess as a tight and tough trio. Songs about public baths, saving trees, milk shakes, and boys named Johnny abound—but not only do they punch with perfect spunk and skill, they exude unswervingly upbeat, driving energy thanks to snug, irresistible guitars and spot-on drums. Together, the Yamano sisters offset their guitars with light, sprightly singing that ranges from whimsical to wistful. And they sing in both English and Japanese, so pick your power puff (it might be strawberry cream). It's a do-it-yourself band: Naoko writes lyrics and music; Atsuko designs stage costumes and album cover art. After four self-produced albums, major debut *Let's Knife* was released worldwide in 1992. It's toured with grunge pioneer Nirvana (Kurt Cobain was an ardent fan) in the United States and the UK. Shonen Knife has had a long working relationship with Thurston Moore (Sonic Youth) and also worked with the Presidents of the United States of America. It's covered songs by the Monkees, the Carpenters, Carole King, Ray Davies, and Motown mamas Martha & the Vandellas. It's contributed to a Beach Boys tribute and a Power-puff Girls set. Its collaborators for remixes and artwork have included Stereolab, Towa Tei, and illustrator Yoshitomo Nara. And the list goes on. In 1999, Michie left the band. Much to the relief of "Knife collectors" (as its fans are dubbed), a new lineup was announced in lieu of disbandment: Atsuko, Naoko, and support drummer Mana. Rocking just as consistently and hard as ever (it's been in the biz for twenty-odd years), Shonen Knife has carved a name for itself—and it still slices other acts down to size.

# Siam Shade

MEMBERS Hideki (vocals), Kazuma (guitar, vocals), Daita (guitar), Natin (bass), Junji (drums)
DATES 1993–2002

On December 28, 2001, the five-member Siam Shade stood onstage before 13,000+ fans at a sold-out Nippon Budokan. It was the realization of a dream—and as it turned out, the climax of a career. Two weeks later, Siam Shade's members would announce their disbandment after nine years together. The group arrived in 1994, when self-titled album debut *Siam Shade* hit No. 2 on the indie charts a month after its release, occupying the spot for four weeks as the No. 1 spot changed. Major debut *Siam Shade II* arrived in 1995. By 1996, the band was touring twice a year, touting multiple sold-out shows. Tickets for three days of concerts at Tokyo's Shinjuku Power Station that spring sold out in thirty-six minutes. A stint at NHK hall (capacity: 3,746) filled up that December. And then the band sold out a three-day Liquid Room (3,000 tickets) live in ten minutes. Fronted by clean-cut, fresh-faced vocalist Hideki, Siam Shade looked like the start of a boy-band. But the hardness of its music placed it among the visual acts. It appeared at events sponsored by music magazines like *Vicious* and *Fool's Mate* with more graphic bands such as La'cryma Christi and PIERROT as late as 1998, holding its own in the deluge of makeup, hair, and hair dye. Siam Shade's music is remarkably free flowing, with flashes of bottom-heavy guitar and joyously fancy fingerwork, syncopated beats, and easy-rolling melodies. Hideki's spot-on, youthful vocals meld with perfectly harmonized choruses, whether smoothly mellow or roughed-up just as well as the next hard rocker's. Kazuma and Daita's double guitars lend a Van Halen–Guns N' Roses pizzazz. The band's songs have been used in countless TV dramas and commercials; one of its most famous, "1/3 no junjou na kanjou" (1/3 pure emotion), was used as an ending theme to the anime series *Rurouni Kenshin*. Siam Shade's place in the rock scene is clear. In 1997, it opened for LUNA SEA frontman Ryuichi Kawamura. In May 1999, it contributed to *hide Tribute Spirits*, an album dedicated to the late X JAPAN guitarist; that November, it opened for long-time influence Mötley Crüe. And then there was its charity work. Beginning in 1998, it took part in Act Against AIDS, a charity for which Hideki became an ambassador/liaison. But then Siam Shade decided to break up, playing its last concert before an again-packed Budokan on March 10, 2002.

# Takui

104

| | |
|---|---|
| SUPPORTING MEMBERS | vocals, guitar |
| CONTRIBUTORS | Akio Noyama (guitar), Riu Kato (guitar), Keisuke Okamoto (bass), Ayato Kondo (drums) |
| DATES | CJ de Villar (guitar), Matt Sorum (drums) |
| | 1999– |

No cigarettes. No booze. Sounds like hell to a glam rocker, but punk star Takui (full name: Takui Nakajima) is a health nut, and his music is smartly fresh. He wrote his first song in his early teens, joined his first band in high school in 1994, and went solo in 1999, hosting a slew of radio shows. After full-length debut *Nuclear Sonic Punk* was released in 2000, three mini-albums—2002's *Chunky God Pop*, 2003's *Swanky God Pop*, and *Power To The Music* in 2004—kept the adrenaline pumping. Takui's music comes down to crisp, clean, hard rock, and his singing is that of a young rock 'n' roller, clear, high, and tight with lots of vibrato; alternately, he can growl and grate with the best of them. Rising, rollicking bass lines bolstered by guitar push and pull, simultaneously jiving with deftly harmonized melodies. Grinding, rough "Innovator" is plenty headbangable on *Nuclear Sonic*. But, Takui's style is versatile. *Chunky*'s "Feed Back '78," after being driven by butterfly drums and anticipatory guitar, breaks out into an optimistic, finger-snapping chorus. And *Swanky* closes with "Never Fades Away," a slow, sweet rock ballad that sounds like reflected sunlight. At first, Takui's look was a highly visual one. He wore makeup, donned vinyl pants, and was backed in *Nuclear Sonic Punk* videos by Zilch, the late X JAPAN guitarist hide's Stateside band. He has since moved on to a suit-sporting, streamlined look, and his skill has expanded to earn him the opportunity to work with—and impress—a clutch of Western rockers. Matt Sorum (ex-Guns N' Roses, ex-Cult) drummed on *Nuclear Sonic Punk*. And Takui was crowned "king of punk 'n' roll" and "god of Rock in the new century," respectively, by guitarists CJ de Villar and Stevie Salas. Takui is easy rolling, quick, and independent—and after *Power To The Music*, he took off again, transferring to a new record company and releasing his second full-length album, *VIVAROCK*. Unlike the stereotypical rocker, Takui runs for fun, and his favorite snack is *natto* (fermented soybeans). It all puts him in a prime position to keep up his jumping around, flexible, heartfelt singing, and frenetic guitar playing just the way he likes it—and for as long as he wants.

# Thee Michelle Gun Elephant

MEMBERS   Yusuke Chiba (vocals), Futoshi Abe (guitar), Koji Ueno (bass),
Kazuyuki Kuhara (drums)

DATES   1991–2003

Just so you know, Thee Michelle Gun Elephant's name comes from a former bassist's mispronunciation of the Damned album *Machine Gun Etiquette*, and "Thee" is a tribute to UK punk band Thee Headcoats. A mutual interest in pub and punk rock brought college mates Yusuke Chiba and Futoshi Abe together, and Chiba—uber-serious, super-selective—weeded out what he deemed inadequate musicians for three years before TMGE was declared completely competent in 1991. Five years and an indie album later, TMGE then stated its own case: a raucous, rowdy one, with a few good record makers. Full-length major debut *cult grass stars* was produced by Chris Brown (Radiohead, Elastica); Tom Baker (Beastie Boys) came in for follow-up *High Time*. In 1997, *Chicken Zombies* zoned in at No. 5 on the Japanese charts, followed by a sold-out thirty-six-city, fifty-two-date tour and five UK shows the following year. *Gear Blues* took off by selling over half a million copies in 1998, *Casanova Snake* followed suit in 2000, and in 2001, *Rodeo Tandem Beat Specter* shook up the charts at No. 1. After listening to TMGE, you might feel a little crazy—or "wild-eyed," as one British magazine put it. And that's because you're being hit with whole walls of concentrated, amplified rock. TMGE is noisy like concrete rubbed over granite chunks, causing feedback in your head. Its piles of songs twang and groove, shoving with uncompromising guitar, stretching and crushing multiple senses all at once. With crashing drums, bass lines all over the place, and Chiba's loud, scratchy, gravelly vocals sometimes mixing with, sometimes topping the super-charged mess—it's refreshingly masochistic. Addictive or not, TMGE's brand of melee has spread across the globe. In 1999, TMGE played New York's CBGB and sixteen more shows in the United States. In 2000, it played London, Paris, and a rock festival in France before headlining Japan's Fuji Rock Festival that summer. In 2001, it played the Tibetan Freedom Concert. TMGE decided to call it quits in 2003. But its music stands as a testament to being loud, in your face, and not giving a damn. About anything besides music, TMGE—outfitted in sulk suits, shades, and its stubborn, intensely solid, ear-grinding noise—couldn't have cared less.

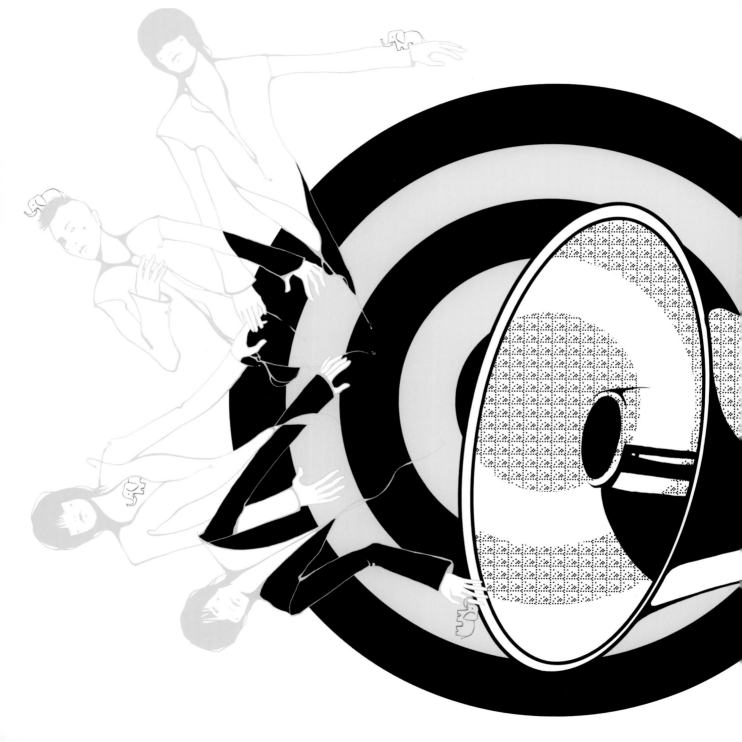

# Unicorn

MEMBERS   Tamio Okuda (vocals, guitar), Isamu Teshima (guitar), Yoshiharu Abe (keyboard), Kazushi Horiuchi (bass), Kohichi Nishikawa (drums)

EX-MEMBER   Midori Mukai (keyboard)

DATES   1985–1993

In 1986, the winner of the Sony music auditions was Unicorn, a five-piece band from Hiroshima. Fronted by vocalist Tamio Okuda, it dressed makeshift punk: scrappy, spunky outfits made of black, patched-up jackets with the sleeves cut off, white t-shirts, and jean shorts. Whatever the expectations were, Unicorn didn't disappoint. Its debut album, synth-seasoned yet sparse *Boom*, sold over 300,000 copies in 1987. After the band switched keyboardists in 1988, single "Daimeiwaku" (Big Trouble) pushed to No.12 on the Oricon in 1989, staying on the charts for two months. Third album *Hattori* kept up the pace, entering at No.10, staying there for three weeks (and on the charts for nearly four months) with over 450,000 copies sold. That July, it played Nippon Budokan. Unicorn's work evolved into deliberately sassy, hilarious songwriting with schizophrenic, mid-song style switches. Okuda's singing can appear completely sober (even sincere) one minute and totally obnoxious the next. On *Hattori*, spoof track "Jinsei wa Joujou da" (Life is the Best!) modulates and keeps modulating; between sparse support tighter than a bug's butt, a messy, egged-on guitar solo, and loopy backup cooing, Okuda's moose-like vocals dissolve into hoarse crack-screaming—and the song doesn't even resolve. Crammed elsewhere on *Hattori* are jazz sprinkles, a sitar, something sounding like a Disney musical soundtrack, and conga-line material that, naturally, transforms into power guitar. (Ukuleles and orchestras are available on other albums.) Like its music, Unicorn's dress comprised everything from kimono and turn-of-the-century suits to regular suits, street clothes, and KISS makeup. But by 1992, all of its members had done some sort of solo work, and their clothing had toned down. After drummer Kohichi Nishikawa left, Unicorn disbanded in September 1993. But its popularity lingered. Two months after the band broke up, compilation album *The Very Best of Unicorn* sold over half a million copies. Today, Unicorn is remembered not only for its skill and place in the Japanese rock scene as an early band, but also for not taking itself too seriously. It put a lot of time into making rock fun—and making fun of rock.

# X JAPAN

MEMBERS  Toshi (vocals), hide (guitar), Pata (guitar), Heath (bass), Yoshiki (piano, drums)
EX-MEMBER  Taiji (bass)
DATES  1985–1997

Think taboo. Think five Madonnas on-stage at the same time. That's the effect X had when it stormed the Japanese indie scene in 1985. Brandishing sky-high blond hair, heavy jagged makeup, and glam rags, members Toshi, Taiji, Pata, hide (pronounced hee-day), and Yoshiki broke equipment, threw instruments, provoked crowds—and the clubs struck back. Not only did hotels and bars lock them out, other bands despised them, and record labels weren't interested, either. Undaunted, Yoshiki founded indie label Extasy Records in 1986, and X's full-length debut, *Vanishing Vision*, was released in 1988. After X held a video giveaway, it landed on TV—branded as comedy—but record companies took note. In 1989, X went major, shoving to No. 6 on the charts with *Blue Blood*. And then it began to set records. In 1991, it performed on the Red and White Music Festival, the first modern rock band to do so. It sold out three consecutive days at the Tokyo Dome the next year. And in 1993, it booked the Dome on New Year's Eve—the venue's most coveted night of the year—for its countdown concert. (In both Tokyo Dome instances, X became the first Japanese artist to usurp honors long dominated by foreign acts.) X seamlessly married classical orchestration to treacherous, '80s-style rock in its songs; a balance of brute force and fleeting beauty was its signature. "Silent Jealousy" first seduces with a glossy, poignant piano solo before launching into raucous, pounding drums and cascading into a waiting ocean of twin guitars. "Blue Blood" breathes with tight tremolos and lyrical lines, Toshi's raspy but emotive vocals cutting through the relentless melee like a scythe. And then there are haunting instrumental pieces like "Love Replica," a twisted, manipulated waltz threaded with cruel guitar. Like its music, X's look was individualistic. Square-shouldered Toshi donned leather and metal, looking like a character out of the anime *Gundam*. Taiji dolled up in perfect, pretty glam. Pata's sleepy, backseat demeanor and whiskey bottle became his trademark, as hide forever goaded the audience. And Yoshiki was a paradox all his own, bewitchingly effeminate one moment—and a full-force, wrist-breaking (literally) hurricane in concert the next. X became a slash-and-burn band, catalyzing the growth of a new movement, visual kei, from the ashes of glam rock. Extasy Records fostered baby talents LUNA SEA and GLAY before they tore up the charts. Side projects went international: hide collaborated with Tommy Aldridge (Whitesnake, Ozzy Osbourne). Yoshiki took time out to work with the London Philharmonic and Roger Taylor (Queen). And on X's final album, *DAHLIA*, the American Symphony contributed to the acoustic version of "Forever Love," theme song for the anime movie X. X planned to go international, too. After changing bassists, it renamed itself X JAPAN, anticipating a U.S. debut. Sadly, Toshi left the band in 1997 and hide died in 1998, preventing those dreams from reaching fruition. A compilation of its pre-*DAHLIA* work, *Best*, was released in North America in 2004.

# Discography

Album names are depicted as they appear on the original official printed materials. Translations sometimes appear in brackets. Date is release date as near as can be determined, in the ISO format (Y-M-D). Asterisks (*) denote mini-albums. Independent releases made after the artist joined a major label are noted in parentheses.

 Nanase Aikawa

MAJOR RELEASES 1996-07-03 *Red*, 1997-07-02 *Paradox*, 1998-07-08 *Crimson*, 2000-02-16 *Foxtrot*, 2001-02-21 *Purana*, 2001-09-27 *The Last Quarter*,* 2004-02-18 *7 seven*, 2005-02-16 *The First Quarter**

COMPILATIONS 1999-05-19 *ID*, 2003-03-26 *ID:2*

OFFICIAL WEB SITES www.nanase.gr.jp, www.avexnet.or.jp/nanase

THE ALFEE

MAJOR RELEASES 1979-08-21 *Time and Tide*, 1980-05-21 *San Juu Shi*, 1981-10-21 *ALMIGHTY*, 1982-04-21 *doubt,*, 1983-01-05 *ALFEE*, 1983-09-05 *ALFEE'S LAW*, 1984-07-05 *THE RENAISSANCE*, 1985-06-19 *FOR YOUR LOVE*, 1986-11-05 *AGES*, 1987-12-09 *U.K. Breakfast*, 1989-03-21 *DNA–Communication–*, 1990-10-17 *ARCADIA*, 1992-04-29 *JOURNEY*, 1995-01-20 *Mugen no Hate ni*, 1996-03-21 *LOVE*, 1998-03-25 *Nouvelle Vague*, 1998-08-07 *Pride*, 1999-09-29 *örb*, 2001-09-12 *GLINT BEAT*, 2003-09-30 *Going My Way*

COMPILATIONS 1983-07-21 *Alfee A-side Collection*, 1983-10-05 *Alfee B-side Collection*, 1983-12-05 *Page One*, 1984-09-05 *ALFEE GOLD*, *ALFEE SILVER*, 1984-12-05 *BEST SELECTION I*, 1985-12-05 *The Best Songs*, 1986-04-21 *Alfee A-side Collection Special*, *Alfee B-side Collection Special*, 1986-12-21 *NON-STOP*, 1987-09-17 *ONE NIGHT DREAMS 1983–1987*, 1988-05-21 *BEST SELECTION II*, 1991-12-04 *THE BEST*, 1992-12-16 *Promised Love*, 1993-07-21 *CONFIDENCE–The Alfee Acoustic Special Live–*, 1994-09-20 *Single History Vol. 1 1978–1982*, 1994-10-20 *Single History Vol. 2 1983–1986*, 1994-11-20 *Single History Vol. 3 1987–1989*, 1995-01-20 *Single History Vol. 4 1990–1994*, 1995-07-21 *LIVE IN PROGRESS*, 1996-12-16 *CLASSICS*, 1996-12-16 *CLASSICS II*, 1997-11-19 *Emotional Message Songs*, 2001-11-16 *CLASSICS III*,

2003-03-05 *THE BEST 1997–2002–apres Nouvelle Vague–*,
2004-08-25 *30th Anniversary Hit Single Collection 37*

www.alfee.com OFFICIAL WEB SITE

BOØWY C

1982-03-21 *Moral*, 1983-09-25 *Instant Love* (indie), 1985-06-21 *BOØWY* (indie),  MAJOR RELEASES
1986-03-01 *Just A Hero* (indie), 1986-11-08 *Beat Emotion* (indie),
1987-09-05 *Psychopath* (indie)

*1988-05-03 Last gigs* (indie), *1988-12-24 Singles* (indie),  COMPILATIONS
1989-12-24 *"Gigs" Just A Hero Tour 1986*, 1991-12-24 *Complete*,
1998-02-25 *This BOØWY*, 2001-11-28 *"Gigs" Case of BOØWY*,
2004-02-24 *Gigs at Budokan*

www.toshiba-emi.co.jp/boowy OFFICIAL WEB SITE

the brilliant green D

1998-09-19 *the brilliant green*, 1999-09-08 *TERRA2001*, 2001-01-11 *Los Angeles*,  MAJOR RELEASES
2002-12-04 *THE WINTER ALBUM*

www.ken-on.co.jp/tbg OFFICIAL WEB SITE

BUCK-TICK

1987-04-01 *HURRY UP MODE* INDIE RELEASE

1987-11-21 *SEXUAL xxxxx!*, 1988-03-21 *ROMANESQUE*,* 1988-06-21 *Seventh Heaven*,  MAJOR RELEASES
1989-01-18 *TABOO*, 1990-02-01 *Aku no Hana* [Evil Flowers],
1991-02-21 *Kurutta Taiyou*, 1992-03-21 *Koroshi no Shirabe This is NOT Greatest Hits*,
1993-06-23 *darker than darkness–style 93–*, 1995-09-21 *Six/Nine*,
1996-06-21 *COSMOS*, 1997-12-10 *SEXY STREAM LINER*, 1998-03-11 *LTD*,*
2000-09-20 *One Life, One Death*, 2002-06-03 *Kyokutou I LOVE YOU*,
2003-02-13 *Mona Lisa Overdrive*

| | |
|---|---|
| COMPILATIONS | 1990-02-08 *HURRY UP MODE (1990MIX)*, 1990-07-21 *Symphonic Buck-Tick in Berlin*, 1994-08-24 *Shapeless*, 1995-12-01 *CATALOGUE 1987–1995*, 1998-08-12 *SWEET STRANGE LIVE DISK* (live album), 1999-03-20 *BT*, 2000-03-29 *97BT99*, 2001-03-28 *One Life, One Death Cut Up* (live album), 2001-12-19 *Super Value Buck-Tick*, 2004-04-07 *at the night side* (live album) |
| OFFICIAL WEB SITE | www.buck-tick.com |

**E  B'z**

| | |
|---|---|
| MAJOR RELEASES | 1988-09-21 *B'z*, 1989-05-21 *OFF THE LOCK*, 1990-02-21 *BREAKTHROUGH*, 1990-11-07 *RISKY*, 1991-11-27 *IN THE LIFE*, 1992-10-28 *RUN*, 1994-03-02 *The 7th Blues*, 1995-11-22 *LOOSE*, 1997-11-19 *SURVIVE*, 1999-07-14 *Brotherhood*, 2000-12-06 *ELEVEN*, 2002-07-03 *GREEN*, 2003-09-17 *BIG MACHINE* |
| COMPILATIONS | 1998-05-20 *B'z The Best "Pleasure,"* 1998-09-20 *B'z The Best "Treasure,"* 2000-02-23 *B'z The "Mixture,"* 2002-12-11 *The Ballads~Love & B'z~* |
| OFFICIAL WEB SITES | www.bz-vermillion.com, www.being.co.jp/bz |

**Cocco**

| | |
|---|---|
| MAJOR RELEASES | 1997-05-21 *Bouganvillea*, 1998-05-13 *Kumuiuta*, 2000-06-14 *Rapunzel*, 2001-04-18 *Sangrose* |
| COMPILATION | 2001-09-05 *Best Album* |
| OFFICIAL WEB SITE | www.cocco.co.jp |

**Dir en grey**

| | |
|---|---|
| INDIE RELEASE | 1997-07-25 *MISSA* |
| MAJOR RELEASES | 1999-07-28 *GAUZE*, 2000-09-20 *MACABRE*, 2002-01-30 *kisou*, 2002-07-31 *six Ugly*,* 2003-09-10 *VULGAR*, 2005-03-09 *Withering to death.* |
| OFFICIAL WEB SITE | www.direngrey.co.jp |

**Dué le quartz**

1999-11-21 *Mikansei Jekyll to Hyde*\* [The Unfinished Story of Jekyll and Hyde],
2000-05-28 *Jisatsu Ganbou*\* [Suicidal Wish], 2002-05-12 *rodeo*,
2002-09-04 *LAST TITLE*
2002-09-04 *BEST ALBUM*

**Duel Jewel**
2001-08-22 *Lapidary*, 2002-09-25 *Noah*\*
www.dueljewel.net

**Gackt**
1999-05-12 *Mizerable,*\* 2000-04-26 *MARS*, 2001-04-18 *Rebirth*, 2002-06-19 *MOON*,
2003-12-03 *Crescent*, 2005-02-14 *Love Letter*
2004-02-25 *The Sixth Day*, 2004-05-26 *The Seventh Night*
www.dears.ne.jp, www.crownrecord.co.jp/gackt.htm

**GLAY**
1994-05-25 *Hai to Daiyamondo* [Ash and Diamond]
1995-03-01 *SPEED POP*, 1996-02-07 *BEAT out!*, 1996-11-18 *BELOVED*,
1998-07-29 *pure soul*, 1999-10-20 *HEAVY GAUGE*, 2001-11-28 *ONE LOVE*,
2002-09-19 *UNITY ROOTS & FAMILY, AWAY*, 2004-03-24 *THE FRUSTRATED*
1997-10-01 *REVIEW*, 1998-02-25 *GLAY SONG BOOK*, 2000-11-29 *GLAY DRIVE*,
2003-02-05 *rare collectives vol. 1, rare collectives vol. 2*
www.glay.co.jp/en/index.html

**hide**
1994-02-23 *Hide Your Face*, 1996-09-02 *Psyence*,
with Spread Beaver: 1998-11-21 *Ja, Zoo*

| | |
|---|---|
| COMPILATIONS | 1997-06-21 *tune up/hide remixes*, 2000-03-02 *hide BEST~PSYCOMMUNITY~*, 2002-05-22 *Psy-Clone~hide Electronic Remixes~*, 2002-07-24 *hide SINGLES–Junk Story–* |
| OFFICIAL WEB SITES | odn.m-up.com/hide, www.hide-city.com |

### H Janne Da Arc

| | |
|---|---|
| INDIE RELEASES | 1998-04-17 *Dearly*,* 1998-12-05 *Resist*,* 1999-03-17 *CHAOS MODE*,* 2000-03-08 *D.N.A.*, 2001-02-28 *Z-HARD*, 2002-01-23 *Gaia*, 2003-02-13 *Another Story*, 2004-07-07 *Arcadia* |
| COMPILATIONS | 2003-09-18 *Singles*, *Another Singles* |
| OFFICIAL WEB SITE | www.janne.co.jp |

### I Judy And Mary

| | |
|---|---|
| INDIE RELEASE | 1992.04 *Be Ambitious* |
| MAJOR RELEASES | 1994-01-21 *J.A.M*, 1994-12-01 *Orange Sunshine*, 1995-12-04 *Miracle Diving*, 1997-03-26 *The Power Source*, 1998-06-27 *Pop Life*, 2001-02-07 *Warp* |
| COMPILATIONS | 2000-03-23 *Fresh*, 2001-05-23 *The Great Escape* |
| OFFICIAL WEB SITE | www.sonymusic.co.jp/eng/Arch/JudyAndMary |

### Kagrra,

| | |
|---|---|
| INDIE RELEASES AS KAGGRA | 2000-12-01 *Nue*,* 2001-03-03 *Sakura*,* 2001-10-03 *Irodori*,* 2002-05-01 *Kirameki** [Shine], 2002-12-11 *Gozen*,* 2003-09-24 *Ouka Ranman** [Sakura in Full Bloom] |
| MAJOR RELEASE AS KAGGRA, OFFICIAL WEB SITE | 2004-03-03 *Miyako* www.pscompany.co.jp/kagrra, |

### J Kuroyume

| | |
|---|---|
| INDIE RELEASES | 1992-12-25 *Ikiteita Chuuzetsuji* [Aborted Living Fetus], 1993-06-11 *Nakigara wo...* [Corpse...] |

1994-03-09 *Mieru Yuritachi~Romance of Scarlet~*, 1994-08-31 *Cruel*,* MAJOR RELEASES
1995-05-10 *Feminism*, 1996-05-29 *Fake Star–I'm Just A Japanese Fake Rocker–*,
1997-06-27 *Drug Treatment*, 1998-05-27 *Corkscrew*
1998-01-01 *1997.10.31 LIVE AT Shinjuku Loft*, COMPILATIONS
1999-02-17 *EMI 1994–1998 BEST OR WORST*, 2002-03-27 *Singles*,
2003-09-29 *Complete Singles*
<u>www.kiyoharu.jp</u> OFFICIAL WEB SITE

La'cryma Christi
1996-02-01 *Warm Snow*,* 1996-07-01 *Dwellers of a Sandcastle** INDIE RELEASES
1997-11-12 *Sculpture of Time*, 1998-11-25 *Lhasa*, 2000-03-15 *magic theatre*, MAJOR RELEASES
2002-03-06 *&U*, 2003-11-05 *DEEP SPACE SYNDICATE*
2000-06-28 *Single Collection*, 2004-09-08 *GREATEST-HITS* COMPILATIONS
<u>www.lacrymachristi.jp</u> OFFICIAL WEB SITE

L'Arc~en~Ciel
1993-04-27 *DUNE* INDIE RELEASE
1994-07-14 *Tierra*, 1995-09-01 *heavenly*, 1996-12-12 *True*, 1998-02-25 *HEART*, MAJOR RELEASES
1999-07-01 *ark*, 1999-07-01 *ray*, 2000-08-30 *REAL*, 2004-03-31 *SMILE*
2001-03-14 *Clicked Singles Best 13*, 2002-06-28 *ectomorphed works*, COMPILATIONS
2003-03-19 *The Best of L'Arc~en~Ciel 1994–1998*,
*The Best of L'Arc~en~Ciel 1998–2000*, *The Best of L'Arc~en~Ciel c/w*
<u>www.larc-en-ciel.com</u> OFFICIAL WEB SITE

LOVE PSYCHEDELICO
2001-01-11 *THE GREATEST HITS*, 2002-01-19 *LOVE PSYCHEDELIC ORCHESTRA*, MAJOR RELEASES
2004-02-25 *LOVE PSYCHEDELICO III*
<u>www.lovepsychedelico.net</u> OFFICIAL WEB SITE

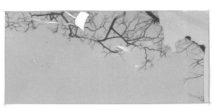  

K  **LUNA SEA**

INDIE RELEASE · 1991-04-21 *Luna Sea*

MAJOR RELEASES · 1992-05-21 *Image*, 1993-04-21 *Eden*, 1994-10-26 *Mother*, 1996-04-22 *Style*,
1998-07-23 *Shine*, 2000-07-12 *Lunacy*

COMPILATIONS · 1997-12-17 *SINGLES*, 1999-05-29 *NEVER SOLD OUT*,
2000-12-23 *Period–The Best Selection–*,
2002-03-06 *Another Side of "SINGLES II"*

OFFICIAL WEB SITE · www.lunasea.co.jp


**Malice Mizer**

INDIE RELEASES · 1994-07-24 *memoire*, 1996-06-09 *Voyage–sans retour–*

MAJOR RELEASES · 1998-03-18 *merveilles*
2000-08-23 *Bara no Seidou* [Rose Sanctuary] (indie)

OFFICIAL WEB SITE · www.malice-mizer.co.jp


**Miyavi**

INDIE RELEASES · 2002-10-31 *gagaku*, 2003-12-02 *Galyuu*

OFFICIAL WEB SITE · www.o-re-sa-ma.com


**Mr. Children**

MAJOR RELEASES · 1992-05-10 *Everything*,* 1992-12-01 *Kind of Love*, 1993-09-01 *versus*,
1994-09-01 *Atomic Heart*, 1996-06-24 *Shinkai* [Deep Sea],
1997-03-05 *Bolero*, 1999-02-03 *Discovery*, 2000-09-27 *Q*,
2002-05-10 *It's a Wonderful World*,
2004-04-07 *Shifuku no Oto* [Sound of Shifuku]

COMPILATIONS · 1999-09-08 *1/42*, 2001-07-11 *Mr. Children 1992–1995*,
2001-07-11 *Mr. Children 1996–2000*

OFFICIAL WEB SITE · www.mrchildren.jp

Penicillin

INDIE RELEASES
1994-05-30 *Penicillin Shock*,* 1994-12-04 *Missing Link*, 1995-06-20 *God of grind** 
1995-09-30 *Earth*,* 1995-09-30 *Into the Valley of Dolls** (indie), 1996-06-26 *Vibe*, MAJOR RELEASES
1996-07-24 *Indwell*,* 1997-07-02 *Limelight*, 1998-10-21 *Ultimate Velocity*,
2000-05-24 *Union Jap*, 2001-11-07 *Nuclear Banana*, 2002-10-30 *No. 53*,
2003-10-01 *Kakkaku*, 2004-10-20 *Flower Circus*
1999-10-06 *THIS IS PENICILLIN 1994–1999*, 2001-02-21 *SINGLES* COMPILATIONS
www.penicillin.jp OFFICIAL WEB SITE

PIERROT

1994-12-01 *Kikurui Piero*, 1996-07-21 *Pandora no Hako* [Pandora's Box], INDIE RELEASES
1997-09-03 *Celluloid**
1999-07-07 *FINALE*, 2000-11-22 *Private Enemy*, MAJOR RELEASES
2002-04-24 *Heaven~The Customized Landscape~*, 2003-07-23 *ID ATTACK*,
2004-12-01 *FREEZE*
2003-12-17 *Dictators Circus–Kijutsuteki Senritsu–* OTHER RELEASE
www.pierrot-web.jp OFFICIAL WEB SITE

the pillows

1990-05-21 *Pantomine*,* 1990-10-25 *90's My Life** INDIE RELEASES
1991-06-21 *Moon Gold*, 1992-05-21 *White Incarnation*, 1994-07-02 *Kool Spice*, MAJOR RELEASE
1995-03-24 *Living Field*, 1997-01-22 *Please Mr. Lostman*, 1998-02-21 *Little Busters*,
1999-01-22 *Runners High*, 1999-12-02 *Happy Bivouac*, 2001-10-31 *Smile*,
2002-10-23 *Thank you, my twilight*, 2003-11-06 *Penalty Life*,
2004-11-03 *Good Dreams*
2001-02-07 *Fool on the planet*, 2002-10-23 *Another morning, Another pillows* COMPILATIONS
2004-06-23 *Turn Back*
pillows.gr.jp OFFICIAL WEB SITE

### Princess Princess

MAJOR RELEASES
1986-05-21 *Kiss De Crime*,* 1987-05-21 *TELEPORTATION*,
1988-02-26 *HERE WE ARE*, 1988-11-21 *LET'S GET CRAZY*, 1989-11-17 *"LOVERS,"*
1990-12-21 *PRINCESS PRINCESS*, 1991-12-07 *DOLLS IN ACTION*,
1993-01-21 *Bee-Beep*, 1993-12-22 *[Majestic]*, 1994-08-25 *PRESENTS*,
1995-12-13 *The Last Princess*

COMPILATIONS
1992-07-15 *SINGLES 1987–1992*, 1996-02-01 *The Greatest Princess*,
2001-12-05 *STAR BOX EXTRA PRINCESS PRINCESS*

### M Psycho le Cému

INDIE RELEASES
2001-09-26 *Doppelganger~mou hitori jibun~* [Doppelganger~another me~],
2002-07-17 *Prism**

MAJOR RELEASES
2003-08-27 *FRONTIERS*, 2004-11-10 *Beautiful World*

OFFICIAL WEB SITE
www.psycholecemu.jp

### N Sheena Ringo

MAJOR RELEASES
1999-02-24 *Muzai Moratorium*, 2000-03-31 *Shoso Strip*,
2002-09-13 *Utaite Myouri* (cover album),
2003-02-23 *Karuki Zamen Kuri no Hana* [Chlorine, Semen, Chestnut Flower]

OFFICIAL WEB SITE
www.toshiba-emi.co.jp/ringo/english

### O SADS

MAJOR RELEASES
1999-09-22 *SAD BLOOD ROCK 'N ROLL*, 2000-06-07 *BABYLON*,
2001-08-29 *THE ROSE GOD GAVE ME*, 2002-04-12 *untitled* (indie),
2003-03-26 *13*

COMPILATION
2003-07-09 *GREATEST HITS–BEST OF 5 YEARS–*

OFFICIAL WEB SITE
www.kiyoharu.jp

## SEX MACHINEGUNS

P

1998-10-16 *Sex Machinegun*, 1999-11-26 *Made In Japan*, 2001-03-07 *Barbe-Q Michael*, 2002-10-09 *Ignition*, 2005-03-02 *HEAVY METAL THUNDER* — MAJOR RELEASES

2001-10-31 *Burning Hammer* (live album), 2003-06-04 *MACHINEGUNS GET-TOGETHER*, 2003-09-26 *Live! Final Attack at BUDOKAN* — COMPILATIONS

2003-08-06 *To the future tracks* — OTHER RELEASE

www.sexmachineguns.com — OFFICIAL WEB SITE

## SHAZNA

Q

1994-11-30 *Sophia,** 1996-03-14 *Melty Case,** 1996-08-01 *Raspberry Time,** 1997-01-22 *Promise Eve** — INDIE RELEASES

1998-01-22 *Gold Sun and Silver Moon*, 1999-06-30 *Pure Hearts* — MAJOR RELEASES

2000-01-01 *OLDIES* — COMPILATION

## SHEENA & THE ROKKETS

1979-03-25 *#1*, 1979-10-25 *Shinkuu Pakku* [Empty Pack], 1980-10-21 *Channel Good*, 1981-09-05 *Pinup Baby Blues*, 1984-11-21 *New Hippies*, 1985-05-21 *Main Songs*, 1986-06-21 *Gathered*, 1986-12-16 *Captain Guitar And Baby Rock*, 1987-09-21 *#9*, 1988-07-21 *Happy House*, 1989-08-21 *Dream+Revolt*, 1992-06-23 *(Ha! Ha! Ha!) Hard Drug*, 1994-04-21 *ROCK ON BABY*, 1997-08-06 *@Heart*, 2000-08-09 *Rock The Rock* — MAJOR RELEASES

2003-07-02 *Dream BOX* — COMPILATION

www.rokkets.com — OFFICIAL WEB SITE

## Shonen Knife

R

1983-07-21 *Burning Farm*, 1984-05-25 *Yama no Attchan*, 1986-06-20 *PRETTY LITTLE BAKA GUY*, 1991-07-01 *712* — INDIE RELEASES

| | |
|---|---|
| MAJOR RELEASES | 1992-08-26 *Let's Knife*, 1993-09-08 *Rock Animals*, 1996-08-21 *Brand New Knife*, 1998-06-24 *Happy Hour*, 2000-02-19 *Strawberry Sound*, 2002-05-23 *Heavy Songs*, 2003-05-22 *Candy Rock* |
| COMPILATIONS | 1992-12-02 *Do The Knife*, 1995-02-22 *GREATEST HISTORY*, 1996-03-05 *The Birds and the B-sides* |
| OTHER RELEASES | 1994-03-02 *Favorites*, 1997-01-22 *Super Mix*, 1997-04-23 *IT'S A NEW FIND*, 1997-10-22 *Ultra Mix* |
| OFFICIAL WEB SITE | www.shonenknife.net |

## Siam Shade

| | |
|---|---|
| INDIE RELEASE | 1994-12-10 *Siam Shade* |
| MAJOR RELEASES | 1995-11-11 *Siam Shade II*, 1996-10-02 *Siam Shade III*, |
| COMPILATIONS | 1998-01-21 *Siam Shade IV*, 1998-12-02 *Siam Shade V*, 2000-07-26 *Siam Shade VI*, 2000-11-29 *Siam Shade VII*,\* 2002-01-30 *Siam Shade VIII—B-side Collection*, 2002-03-06 *Siam Shade IX—A-side Collection*, 2002-11-27 *Siam Shade X—The Perfect Collection* |
| OFFICIAL WEB SITES | www.amuse.co.jp/news/siamshade www.sonymusic.co.jp/Music/Arch/SMER/SiamShade |

## s Takui

| | |
|---|---|
| MAJOR RELEASES | 2000-10-25 *Nuclear Sonic Punk*, 2002-06-19 *Chunky God Pop*,\* 2002-10-23 *Swanky God Pop*,\* 2004-02-25 *Power To The Music*\* (indie), 2004-09-23 *VIVAROCK* |
| OFFICIAL WEB SITE | www.takui.com |

## t Thee Michelle Gun Elephant

| | |
|---|---|
| INDIE RELEASE | 1995-10-21 *Wonder Style*\* |

1996-03-01 *cult grass stars*, 1996-11-01 *High Time*, 1997-11-01 *Chicken Zombies*, MAJOR RELEASES
1998-11-25 *Gear Blues*, 2000-03-01 *Casanova Snake*,
2001-05-23 *Rodeo Tandem Beat Specter*, 2003-03-05 *Sabrina Heaven*,
2003-06-21 *Sabrina no Heaven**
1999-08-06 *RUMBLE*, 2000-12-13 *TMGE106*, COMPILATIONS
2002-12-25 *The Grateful Triad Years 1995–2002*
2000-12-13 *Casanova said "Live or Die,"* 2003-12-03 *LAST HEAVEN'S Bootleg* OTHER RELEASES
www.tmge.co.jp, www.rockin-blues.com OFFICIAL WEB SITES

Unicorn
1987-10-21 *Boom*, 1988-07-21 *Panic Attack*, 1989-06-01 *Hattori*, MAJOR RELEASES
1990-10-01 *Kedamono no Arashi* [Storm of Wild Beasts],
1990-11-01 *Odoru Kameya Bushi*,* 1990-12-01 *Have a Nice Day*,*
1991-09-30 *Hige to Boin* [Beard and Big Tits],
1993-01-21 *Unicorn/EbiOkudaAbeNishikawaTeshima*, 1993-05-21 *Springman*
1992-02-21 *Oldies But Goldies ~ Unicorn's Selection*, COMPILATIONS
1993-11-21 *The Very Best of Unicorn*, 1994-04-21 *The Very Rust of Unicorn*,
1995-12-13 *UNICORN Golden Half Special*, 1999-01-30 *Star Box Unicorn*,
2002-12-18 *Ultra Super Golden Wonderful Special*

X JAPAN ᴜ
1988-04-14 *Vanishing Vision* INDIE RELEASE
1989-04-21 *Blue Blood*, 1991-07-01 *Jealousy*, 1993-08-25 *Art of Life** MAJOR RELEASES
1996-11-04 *DAHLIA*
1993-11-21 *X Singles*, 1996-12-01 *B.O.X~Best of X~*, 1997-12-19 *Ballad Collection*, COMPILATIONS
1997-12-25 *Singles~Atlantic Years~*, 1999-02-24 *Perfect Best*, 2001-09-05 *Star Box*
2004-02-24 *Best* (North America) OTHER RELEASE
www.xjapan.ne.jp OFFICIAL WEB SITE